*To Michel –
I hope this finds
you well. Please
let me know if you
are ever in Vancouver.*

On
*To future
memories*

Susan

Landscapes

"*On Landscapes* takes a fresh, contemporary look at the ever-important topic of landscapes. Herrington mixes impressive knowledge and expertise with a clear, accessible style, using a range of cutting-edge examples from everyday landscapes to grand gardens. The coverage is admirable, and the author's discussion of both historical and contemporary ideas provides useful knowledge and context concerning the evolution of this type of environment."

Emily Brady, University of Edinburgh

"The strength of *On Landscapes* lies in its accessibility and the interesting range of projects chosen from a diverse selection of historical periods and cultural locations. The writing style is lucid and wonderfully rich, which makes for a really engaging as well as visually stimulating book."

Jane Rendell, Bartlett School of Architecture,
University College London

Susan Herrington is an Associate Professor of landscape architecture and environmental design at the University of British Columbia. She is also a licensed landscape architect in the United States.

D1292174

Praise for the series

SUSAN HERRINGTON

On
Landscapes

Routledge
Taylor & Francis Group

NEW YORK AND LONDON

First published 2009
by Routledge
270 Madison Ave, New York, NY 10016

Simultaneously published in the UK
by Routledge
2 Park Square, Milton Park, Abingdon, Oxon OX14 4RN

Routledge is an imprint of the Taylor & Francis Group, an informa business

© 2009 Taylor & Francis

Typeset in Joanna MT and DIN by
RefineCatch Limited, Bungay, Suffolk
Printed and bound in the United States of America on acid-free paper by
Edwards Brothers, Inc

Trademark Notice: Product or corporate names may be trademarks or registered
trademarks, and are used only for identification and explanation without intent to
infringe.

Library of Congress Cataloging-in-Publication Data
Herrington, Susan.
  On landscapes / by Susan Herrington.
    p. cm.—(Thinking in action)
  Includes bibliographical references.
  1. Landscape.   I. Title.
  BH301.L3H37 2008
  712'.2—dc22   2008009268

ISBN10: 0–415–99124–2 (hbk)
ISBN10: 0–415–99125–0 (pbk)

ISBN13: 978–0–415–99124–7 (hbk)
ISBN13: 978–0–415–99125–4 (pbk)

For Dominic McIver Lopes

Landscape is the hidden art. It's everywhere and it's part of everyone's life. It isn't closeted in a museum or concert hall. Nevertheless, it doesn't get the same level of sustained attention as the arts, like painting and music, that we can choose to ignore. This book is about how to see the invisible.

To do that, a traditional approach won't work, so this book is not a history of landscapes, although some historical landscapes are discussed. The landscapes you will read about look quite different from traditional landscapes. They are not scenes of green rolling hills punctuated by trees and calm lakes, and they are certainly not places where aristocrats, sporting silk coats and breeches, stroll about. At the same time these new landscapes build upon the past, inviting memory, imagination, and anticipation.

You will travel to a quirky private garden in Boston, to post-industrial parks in the U.K. and Germany, to an unexpected rest stop in France, and to a former garbage dump turned into a park for play in Japan. Many contemporary landscapes are industrial sites—former factories, land fills, and ports—made over. They are the remnants of the industrial West, and they turn the challenges of the industrial past into opportunities for the future.

They also grow out of changes in how we think about art and nature. The modern era distrusted deception in art.

Twentieth-century painting, for example, stressed that painting is paint, and not illusion. Many contemporary landscapes reveal themselves as constructions and are not disguised as untouched nature. Also, since we now recognize that nature constantly changes, these landscapes are designed to display this change.

Finally, landscapes have come to represent a process of reflection. Artists, landscape architects, and designers question what landscapes are and what they mean. Landscapes that reflect on the nature of landscapes can help us see what they are about. So this is where we begin.

Many individuals graciously gave their time to the improvement of the manuscript. I thank Allen Carlson, Gina Crandell, Marcella Eaton, Lisa Gelfand, Gert Groening, Lesley Johnstone, Dominic McIver Lopes, and Marc Treib for reading and making suggestions on the entire manuscript. I also thank the anonymous reviewers assigned by Routledge for their pointed advice, and the helpful encouragement of Kate Ahl at Routledge. With the generous permission of the University of Wisconsin Press, several paragraphs in the sections on memory and narrative are reproduced from my papers "Framed Again" and "Gardens Can Mean" in *Landscape Journal*. I am also very thankful to the people who allowed me to reproduce their images in this book: Bridget Baines at Gross Max, Claude Cormier at Claude Cormier Architectes Paysagistes, D. James Dee and Ronald Feldman Fine Arts, Luca M. F. Fabris, Field Operations and Diller Scofidio + Renfro and The City of New York, Mike Forsyth at Calligrafix, Professor Bernard Lassus at Atelier Bernard Lassus, Michael Latz, Dominic McIver Lopes, Kate B. Notman at Ryan Associates, Danya Sherman at the Friends of the High Line, Joel Sternfeld, Alan Ward at Sasaki Associates and Erin Leitzes at Martha Schwartz Partners, and Peter Wouda at www.timesfoundation.com. Lastly, I am particularly grateful to Dominic McIver Lopes and Turner Wigginton who consistently provided their support during the writing of this book.

LIKE CHOCOLATE FOR WATER
The Bagel Garden

Among the orderly procession of front yards that appoints nineteenth-century homes in the Back Bay neighborhood of Boston, Martha Schwartz created the Bagel Garden. Like its neighbors, a clipped boxwood hedge bordered the garden. Yet, in contrast to what you might expect to find cradled in this shady residential yard—a brick patio, blooming roses, a small bubbling fountain—the hedge enclosed 96 lacquered bagels (a mixture of salt and pumpernickel). These bagels were not accessories to a garden scene, placed in a bowl gracing a table. Instead, they were brazenly laid out in a grid pattern upon a ground of colored gravel.

While the Bagel Garden didn't look like other gardens in her neighborhood, Schwartz argued that it was a garden. Proclaiming that bagels were perfect for her north facing small urban site, she noted that they were shade tolerant, inexpensive, locally available, and required little maintenance. Although the Back Bay Garden Club placed the Garden on its itinerary of educational tours, many argued that it was not a garden because its main features were not plants. Schwartz professed that she liked plants, but in some locations, plants were too difficult to maintain. "Having a landscape is like

Figure 0.1 Martha Schwartz, The Bagel Garden (photo credit: © Alan Ward Photograph)

having a pet. You have to feed it. If you can't, get a stuffed animal."[1]

The Bagel Garden appeared on the January 1980 cover of *Landscape Architecture* magazine and in that year almost every issue of the magazine contained letters of complaint as well as praise for the garden. Many landscape architects were appalled. They protested that Schwartz was not contributing anything to society or the profession with her sensational work.

But what makes it so difficult to accept these simple ring-shaped bread rolls as part of a garden?

Not all gardens feature plants. In fact, one of the most highly respected gardens in the world, Ryoan-ji in Kyoto, has very little vegetation. Ryoan-ji is an enclosed courtyard containing 15 rocks placed in drifts of moss that rest on a bed of raked gravel. It is considered a quintessential example of Japan's traditional dry garden (kare-sansui), thought to aid monks in the meditation rituals associated with Zen Buddhism.

Granted, there are remarkable differences between the two gardens. The Bagel Garden was temporary (lasting only a few months) and it was located in a vernacular landscape—the front yard. In contrast, Ryoan-ji is said to have been built in 1499 and is located within the sacred precinct of a Buddhist temple complex. However, there are also similarities. Like the Bagel Garden, plants are not the most prominent feature. Also

Figure 0.2 Ryoan-ji (photo credit: Susan Herrington)

like the Bagel Garden, it is an enclosed, rectilinear space that is to be looked at rather than moved through with the body.

But if the Bagel Garden is a kind of garden, how can it help us answer the question—what are landscapes?

Gardens are often mistakenly discounted from discussions about landscapes. Yet, historically, they have been the testing grounds for new ideas that were later applied to landscapes. For example, André le Nôtre's garden design for Vaux-le-Vicomte in the seventeenth century served as a model for the urban development of Paris for the next 300 years.[2] His experimentation with the vanishing point of the grand axis at Vaux provided the template for the axial scenography linking the Louvre, Tuileries, Arc de Triomphe, and La Grande Arche. This is now a signature of the Parisian landscape, but it began with experiments in a garden.

The garden historian John Dixon Hunt notes that "gardens focus the art of place-making or landscape architecture in the way that poetry can focus the art of writing. Not everyone wants to write poetry, nor do its modes of expression suit every occasion or topic."[3] By the turn of a word or phrase, poetry can question the conventions and expectations of writing, and what writing is. Schwartz's experimental garden raises important questions about landscapes. Who designs landscapes? What can they represent? And are they natural? These questions comprise the first part of this book.

Authorship

Although landscapes are created by humans, many landscapes conceal this human intervention. Schwartz's garden with its grid of bagels brazenly calls attention to the fact that it was designed by a human. It signals that the Bagel Garden is not naturally occurring. Bagels will never, and have never, sprouted from the ground on their own accord. Neither is the bagel grid a result of neglect. It is not what we would expect to find had her yard been abandoned for years. As a consequence, the garden does not present us with what might have 'originally' occupied that spot of land outside of Schwartz's house.

The question of landscape authorship has been contested for a long time. Many landscapes contain natural elements and are subject to natural processes that obscure human intervention. The nineteenth-century antiquarian Quatremère de Quincy maintained that landscape gardens that looked indistinguishable from what nature produced could not be considered art. This view influenced the unbridled beautification of Victorian landscapes that stressed the very human artifice of garden making. Neatly shaved lawns punctuated by mass-produced ornaments, the technicolor of exotic flowers, and topiary carved into motifs limited only by the imagination clearly signaled their human authorship and thus their claims to status as an artistic practice.

Despite all this well intended artifice, neither gardens or landscapes were unanimously accepted as art. During the following century, landscapes became valued for what modern art rejected—representing nature or some lost human state in nature. As a result, signs of human authorship in the design of landscapes were often disguised. Artificial stone was carefully crafted to simulate rock outcrops, soil was imported and shaped to mimic the land forms left by some long-departed glacier, and vegetation was installed to resemble naturally occurring ecosystems, such as meadows.

Representation

Gardens often represent historical myths regarding human life and creation. It is thought that the Ryoan-ji rocks refer to mountainous islands, while the raked gravel denotes water, perhaps a sea. In this way, Ryoan-ji represents a natural formation—one produced by the processes of colliding tectonic plates and the upward thrust of volcanic mountains. But it also refers to a Chinese garden myth begun by Han Dynasty Emperor Han Wu Ti, initiating one of the world's oldest garden conventions of rock and water.

Emperors before Wu Ti sent scouts to the East Sea, where steep islands of rock emerged from its turbulent waters. This mysterious landscape of rock and water was home to storks who were said to know the secret of eternal life. Repeated excursions by scouts were unsuccessful in finding the elusive storks, so Han Wu Ti being a pragmatic man, changed the game-plan. He built a garden as a miniature version of the East Sea—a garden of rocks and water—so that he could attract the storks himself.[4] Thus, one interpretation of Ryoan-ji suggests that it represents this myth.

Landscapes also carry messages with contemporary relevance. This is one point of the Bagel Garden. The irony of placing processed food on land that could potentially produce food represents our contemporary relationship with land, not as a source of sustenance, but as space to be organized. Or, consider the bagels themselves. Although bagels were invented in the seventeenth century, they continue to be the food-stuff of people's real, commercially mediated lives. In this way, the Bagel Garden represents contemporary life, and the fact that landscapes are market driven, swayed by desire, and subject to the anxious acts of consumption.

Nature

People often identify landscapes with nature. One reason for this is that many landscapes in the twentieth century were designed to look like they were purely the result of external, natural processes. In North America this naturalistic style is pervasive. The architectural historian Marc Treib observes that "public green spaces, particularly in the United States, came to rely almost exclusively on the vocabulary of naturalism . . . so complete was its dominance that it remained unquestioned."[5] Moreover, this naturalness has moral overtones. Nature is viewed as good, morally innocent, and so natural-looking landscapes take on the appearance of goodness. This, according to John Dixon Hunt, pitted natural looking gardens as "goodies" against formal looking gardens as "baddies," such that "we fail to see that Prospect Park was just as contrived, just as factitious a mode of laying out grounds as Versailles had been."[6]

Western culture has tried to understand our relationship with nature in different ways. While some contend that we are nature, it is better to *not* hold this view that we are nature and thus all our actions are natural. Humans create landscapes, so we should identify landscapes as artifice, not as external nature. This idea is reflected in the writing of landscape historian J.B. Jackson, who provided one of the most enduring definitions of landscapes:

> A landscape is not a natural feature of the environment but a *synthetic* space, a man-made system of spaces superimposed on the face of the land, functioning and evolving not according to natural laws but to serve a community.[7]

Jackson's use of the word synthetic highlights a common misconception about landscapes—that they result from only external natural processes. Jackson contends that landscapes can contain naturally occurring features, such as plants growing in a meadow, but once we see the meadow as a view, a resource, or place to graze cattle, it becomes a landscape.[8] As accomplices in all we survey, landscapes are not only created physically, but they can also be made through perception.

But what is the value of revealing all these inelegant truths about landscapes, what is the benefit? A major benefit in revealing that landscapes are not natural is that it includes humans in what they are. It acknowledges our role in their making. Since we do in fact shape landscapes, it makes little sense to pretend that they are purely the result of natural processes.[9]

LANDSCAPES AND TIME
Time

Definitions of landscapes and ideas about nature are intertwined because landscapes often contain and perceptually frame natural systems. Jackson points out that landscapes are made when the processes of nature are accelerated or decelerated by humans.

> A landscape is . . . a space deliberately created to speed up or slow down the process of nature. As Eliade expressed it, it represents man taking upon himself the role of time.[10]

A common complaint about the Bagel Garden is that it's temporary. But aren't all gardens temporary? Consider Ryoan-ji again. Its very existence depends heavily upon human labor—the daily raking of the gravel, the care of the moss, and the removal by hand of fallen leaves, blossoms, plastic wrappers, and other animal droppings. If it did not receive this daily attention, fallen debris, encroaching weeds, and animals would obscure its major features—the gravel pattern and rocks.[11] Ryoan-ji's keepers strive to hide the temporality of the garden by giving it an appearance of timelessness.

Even Brooklyn's Prospect Park, designed in the late nineteenth century by Frederick Law Olmsted and Calvert Vaux, manipulates time. Olmsted and Vaux were asked to design this park in the same pastoral manner as their famed Central Park. The site for Prospect Park was a farm, so the designers could have altered its terrain, installed paths and water features, and then waited several decades for grasses, shrubs, evergreen trees, and then hardwood trees to encroach upon the open farm land. Instead Olmsted and Vaux, as they did at Central Park, transplanted large shrubs and mature hardwoods. Some of these mature trees were repositioned from other parts of the farm, but many were imported from outlying properties. The transplanting process was so substantial that a special tree-moving machine was invented for the park's creation. When Prospect Park was opened to the public, with its groupings of mature trees, it appeared older than it actually was.

Yet, all this toying with our perception of time isn't necessarily a bad thing. Indeed, Jackson's idea of landscape as an order of change against the friction of physical time taps some of the most important and enjoyable, dimensions of being human. These include memory (the past), imagination (the present), and anticipation (the future)—themes that comprise the second part of this book.

Memory

Memory has been a potent source of meaning for landscapes since ancient Greece. The Greeks were adept at mining the power of memory through landscapes. When Greece was reduced to a mere province of the expanding Roman Empire, they used the remnants of their landscape as mnemonic devices to fortify Greek identity and appeal to Rome.[12] The remnants of the agora, the nymphaeum, and the sacred grove were preserved by Rome, but they were also transformed from civic and religious sites to memorial landscapes, venerating Greece's glorious past.

These landscapes became valuable to Romans as well, who appropriated them as emblems of classical culture in their own gardens throughout the Empire and Greece itself. For example, the Athenian Agora, honored as the classical site for democratic assembly, was perpetuated as an outdoor museum in homage to classical values. During the second century B.C.E. a succession of wealthy Roman citizens and Emperors added libraries and other public structures to the Agora, each with the idea of being identified with the classical past.

The connection between landscape and memory was strengthened considerably in the eighteenth century as a result of the growing interest in taste. Since taste is based on experience and is not hard-wired in our brains, it can be cultivated. The more memories you could draw from, the richer your experience with art. Landscapes were prized for their ability to conjure up the past for experience.

Memory continues to play an important role in some of the most captivating landscapes of the twenty-first century. These landscapes include conversions of industrial sites into parks that retain hulking industrial ruins (blast furnaces, cooling towers, and abandoned railway lines) as mnemonic markers of a by-gone way of life. Other contemporary examples include memorial landscapes, which index the intractable mystery of death and elicit intense emotions in their visitors. But to cultivate memory, you must have an imagination.

Instrumental Imagination

Imagination is not a flighty enterprise. It helps us to under-stand how things work and to envision events we can't always witness first-hand. What I call an instrumental imagination of landscapes challenges a disinterestedness engagement with them. Disinterestedness is a philosophical legacy from the eighteenth century and a major contribution of philosopher Immanuel Kant. Kant held that something is beautiful when it gives us pleasure and this pleasure is distinct because it is not based on any interest that we may have in the way it functions.[13] For example, in the disinterested stance, the beauty of a prairie landscape can in no way be related to some knowledge about plant succession or the way it was once used by Native Americans. So why can it not be part of its beauty? A practical understanding of landscapes can be pleasurable and we can enjoy learning how something works.

Instrumental imagination is part of many contemporary landscapes that revive the narrative—one of the oldest types of landscapes. Narrative landscapes date back to the fifteenth century B.C.E. In Egypt, routes for many funeral processions were laid out on an east–west axis. They expressed the trespasses of the soul from life, death, and rebirth by tracing the meta-narrative for these events: the moving sun. Moreover, instrumental imagination helps us interpret landscapes by enabling us to gel meaning from the physical world around us; to see it as a story.

A second type of instrumental imagination is a structural model, which can help us make decisions about large, complex landscapes. Structural models have been employed in the creation of many new infrastructure landscapes where the relationships among humans and biophysical systems, such as the filtration of wastewater, are revealed to people as one of its main features. Nevertheless, it is our experience with landscapes that most powerfully shapes what we believe about them.

Experience

Evolutionary theories, which argue that landscape preference is hard-wired in us, dominate recent thought on landscape experience. It is argued that we prefer landscapes that re-enact experiences from our evolutionary past, particularly experiences related to human survival such as protection from predators. The philosopher Allen Carlson points out that many of these evolutionary arguments are explanatory theories, not justificatory ones.[14] They don't justify why certain landscapes experiences are good for us or if they are great.

Moreover, many evolutionary arguments are based on two-dimensional pictures of landscapes, but we actually move around and through landscapes. Physical landscapes can provide intense sensory experiences that combine movement with what we see, hear, smell, and touch. Landscapes designed for play, in particular, link sense experience with motion.

Because landscapes literally compose the context of daily life—the street, the garden, the park—they are subject to social exchange. To understand this better, it is helpful to consider the philosopher John Dewey's theories of aesthetic experience. In *Art and Experience*, Dewey sought to shift notions about art away from what he called the "beauty parlors of civilization"—namely museums. He thought art should be embedded in daily life where it could be useful to people regardless of age, class, gender, or economy.

Dewey's theories of aesthetic experience also underline an important dimension of landscape experience—how we anticipate landscape change. Since landscapes can transform radically throughout the year or even a day, our anticipation of this change becomes a key feature in the experience. Thus, while evolutionary theories entrench sameness across time and space, Dewey's theory posits change.

You might still wonder—why bother with bagels—why do we need Bagel Gardens? Granted, Schwartz went on to produce numerous equally challenging permanent landscapes, but wouldn't the world be a better place if we didn't have people like Schwartz challenging us to think about what landscapes are?

Her critics asked how her work contributed to society. After all, many landscapes are created in the public realm.

Much art forces a critical evaluation of our systems of beliefs. Dewey thought that our experiences with art should contain an element of resistance.[15] Resistance challenges what we believe. Since belief guides us in thinking about what is certain and probable, and it is the springboard for action, it is vital that our beliefs are challenged and verified. For Dewey, resistance occurs when

> the perceiver as well as the artist has to perceive, meet, and overcome problems; otherwise, appreciation is transient and overweighted with sentiment . . . If people are unable to engage with art in a way that challenges beliefs then this experience can lack significant meaning.[16]

Think of the music radio stations boasting that they will never play a song you have never heard. Clearly they know their market and they play songs that are targeted to a specific group and the music this group prefers. Listeners are not confronted with the music, rather they are passive receptors who "get" what they expect.

Listening to music we are familiar with can often increase enjoyment, but there are times when we need new listening experiences that challenge what we think music is. Imagine listening to a musician who will play songs that you have not heard or who mixes songs across genres, engaging listeners by calling into question what they believe is good music, opening up unrealized possibilities and beliefs.

Resistance is particularly relevant to our understanding of landscapes because they are consistently presented to us in forms that are "overweighted with sentiment." Consider the numerous pictures of landscapes that adorn Kleenex boxes, mugs, and bottles of liquid hand soap. We find no resistance here. We probably don't want to confront resistance in our use of mugs, and there are instances when comfort is fine; nonetheless, landscapes are spaces that condition and are conditioned by cultural and natural systems directly connected to our well-being. If we only want to experience what we believe landscapes to be, we stifle growth. So it is good for us to have some resistance in our experiences with landscapes.

Temporary Gardens

Resistance may account for the rise in landscape and garden festivals in Europe and North America, where confronting received belief is the chief occupation for visitors. Garden festivals such as Chaumont in France, the garden design section at the Chelsea Flower Show in England, Bundesgarten Schau in Germany, and Les Jardins de Métis in Canada are hosting temporary gardens which challenge, defy, and expand people's idea of what a garden is and can be.

For example, Les Jardins de Métis is located on the property of a historic garden in rural Quebec. It attracts thousands of people each year, many of whom come to see the very palpable Edwardian garden originally designed by Elsie Reford. However, visitors are also exposed to a banquet of radical gardens in the temporary festival section. For instance, there is the manic expression of Blue Stick Garden designed by landscape architect Claude Cormier.

Blue Stick is composed of 3500 garden stakes. Each stake is painted blue on three sides and orange on the fourth. Walking into the garden, a rectilinear space defined by the stakes, you are surrounded by blue, the collective hue of the stakes. As you turn to leave and expose your eye to the fourth orange side, the entire garden turns orange. The tangy snap of this garden not only challenges our beliefs about what a garden is, but it is also a counter to one of the most beloved traditions of Edwardian culture, the perennial garden.

Compare Blue Stick with the historic perennial gardens at Hestercombe, England, designed by garden artist Gertrude Jekyll. Cormier both references and rebuffs this great garden as he enlists a number of features that challenge us to overcome what we think a garden is. Both gardens are in debt to the viewer's perceptual response. However, Blue Stick replaces

Figure 0.3 Claude Cormier, Blue Stick Garden (photo credit: Claude Cormier Architectes Paysagistes)

the subjective whim and tender care required by Jekyll's garden with the anonymity of the manufactured sticks. Both gardens draw their inspiration from color theories in art that unite visual perception with visceral reaction. Yet, Cormier substitutes the subtle analogous color schemes that are Jekyll's signature with bold cuts across the color wheel from blue to orange. Lastly, Cormier trades the movement of seasons marked by plant growth in Jekyll's perennial garden with the movement of the body as indexed by the eye and the mind.

Like the Bagel Garden, Blue Stick uses materials as a source of resistance that we must overcome. Alexander Reford, historian and director of Les Jardins de Métis, remarks that you can see the changes on people's faces as they try to understand these festival gardens—some pause in wonderment and amazement, others are completely puzzled. Not all visitors overcome the resistance in these gardens. I watched one visitor with great passion rip up his entry ticket declaring "ce ne sont pas des jardins, ceci n'est pas un paysage!"

These gardens challenge what people believe a landscape to be. They also make evident that they are designed by humans. An underlying strategy in both Cormier and Schwartz's work is a desire to make the landscape visible to people as artifice, an environment artfully shaped by humans. These festival gardens clearly announce landscapes as visible expressions of human design. Who designs landscapes has played a special role in understanding what they are, and in the following chapter I will explain why.

One

THE CULT OF DESIGN
Genius Artist

Landscape architects like Schwartz and Cormier epitomize the freedom and verve of rule-defying artists. This conception of artists was forged during the eighteenth century, particularly by Kant who proposed that artists were distinct from crafts people or entertainers. In his *Critique of Judgment* (1790)[1] Kant distinguished people skilled at making fine tables or telling vivid stories at parties from artists who produced music, poetry, painting, sculpture, architecture, oratory, and landscape gardens.[2] As a consequence, artists were charged to be original rather than imitative, and paradigm makers rather than followers.

Early landscape designers adopted many of these characteristics, particularly their originality. Consider the eighteenth century writer and critic Horace Walpole's description of the famous landscape designer William Kent:

> At that moment appeared Kent, painter enough to taste the charms of landscape, bold and opinionative enough to dare and to dictate, and born with a genius to strike out a great system from the twilight of imperfect essays. He leaped the fence, and saw that all nature was a garden.[3]

Walpole's dramatic description of Kent's appearance upon the history of landscape design is marked not only by Kent's own genius, but the way his genius allows him to strike out and leap beyond the practices of mere mortals. For Walpole, it was Kent's genius that helped create one of the most influential paradigms in landscape architecture, the English landscape garden.

This conception of the genius designer continued well into the nineteenth century with the brilliant career of the first professional landscape architect in the United States, Frederick Law Olmsted. Olmsted anticipated the social and health problems caused by increasingly crowded and polluted industrial cities, and he knew that these problems would be exacerbated with time. Thus, he invented new landscape types that would meet the needs of future generations, producing some of the most visionary projects in North America. These include his design (with architect Calvert Vaux) for Central Park, the first major public park in the United States; Riverside, one of the earliest planned suburban developments; as well as the Emerald Necklace (with Charles Eliot) in Boston, a comprehensive series of parks that solved sanitation problems caused by flooding. Prior to Olmsted, urban park spaces were not linked, suburbs developed incrementally, and flooded parts of the city were avoided instead of managed as park spaces. Olmsted leapt many fences by connecting physical landscapes with human health and well-being that had been previously ignored.

Invented Artist

But what about the clients, for whom landscapes are typically designed? For a long time, tensions have marked client—designer relationships. One of the most notorious of these relationships was that between Lady Sarah Churchill, 1st Duchess of Marlborough, and the architect John Vanbrugh, who was charged to build Blenheim Palace for the Duke of Marlborough in the early eighteenth century. Throughout Vanbrugh's endeavor to design the palace and gardens (with Henry Wise), he disagreed with Lady Sarah at every turn. Where Vanbrugh envisioned a wall, Sarah desired a view; where Sarah asked for a cascade, Vanbrugh created a lake; where Vanbrugh proposed an open space, Sarah placed a monument. Vanbrugh finally resigned, and Sarah completed the project eight years later.

Conflict marked Olmsted's career as well. He resigned several times from his various positions at Central Park. He argued bitterly with many Commissioners on the Park Board, and he eventually wrote "The Spoils of the Park: With a Few Leaves from the Deep-laden Note-books of 'A wholly Unpractical Man'" (1882), a blistering summation of the park's mismanagement. The thrust of Olmsted's critique was that the Commissioners ran the park more like a shady side-business rather than a living work of art for the people of New York. This corrupt mismanagement was not only ruining the art of the park, but degrading Olmsted as an artist. He charged that:

> the only man in its employment competent to advise or direct in matters of landscape-gardening has been degraded to an almost menial position, and this by methods and with manners implying a perfectly definite purpose to prevent him from exercising professional discretion, and to bring his art into contempt.[4]

Both Olmsted and Vanbrugh were plagued by clients who lacked an appreciation of their artistic vision. Yet, during the twentieth century another difficulty emerged. The very conception of a "genius artist" was critiqued. These critiques proposed that great artists were not a product of their own genius, rather their brilliance was invented by certain groups and institutions to regulate norms in society. One of these norms held that the genius artist was male, thus the dismantling of this norm became the focus of feminist theories of art.

In "Why Are There No Great Women Artists?"[5] art historian Linda Nochlin revealed how Western culture failed to acknowledge great female artists in its canon of art history. She contended that "art is not a free, autonomous activity of a super-endowed individual." Rather institutions, such as museums and schools, and forms of patronage deem great art and artists. Since it is their function to maintain their power in society they endorse the constellation of norms that appoint men as great artists. As a result they do not assign great art to women. Feminists advocated for the inclusion of women artists in the canon and compelled historians to reconsider the way they categorized great art of the past. Some feminists sought to include art forms traditionally created by women, such as quilts or domestic gardens.

Within the canon of landscape, males have occupied the role of genius designers, fitting the Kantian picture of artists as original and paradigm making. Although female landscape architects have practiced professionally since the nineteenth century, traditionally they were seen as domestic garden designers, sympathetic social reformers, noble and modest technicians, or community nurturers. These roles are important, but they do not intrude upon the rule-breaking domain of the male artist. The fact that Schwartz is a woman is not an irrelevant variable. It may not be a significant feature in her work, but being female is salient to how she defies the categories traditionally assigned to female landscape designers.

Replacing a traditional residential garden with a garden of commercially produced baked goods—alas not even home-made—challenges the traditional role of women as landscape designers. Historically, residential gardens were the "natural" extensions of women's domestic spheres, but they also provided opportunities for artistic and horticultural experimentation that would have been inappropriate outside the private sphere.[6] Schwartz assumes a role usually limited to a man, the rule-defying artist, but she imports this into a traditional female sphere, the domestic garden. The publication of the Bagel Garden on the cover of a professional magazine not only challenged what landscapes are, but who designs them.

Landscapes of Regulations

The forces of gender and space play only one part in answering the question, who designs landscapes? Landscapes in both the private and public realm are under intense official and unofficial scrutiny. What landscapes contain and how they are maintained are often the purview of such groups as neighborhood associations, authorities, and commissions. These groups generate by-laws, ordinances, and technical codes that dictate numerous features from the types of plants landscapes may contain to the height of hand rails. Many official codes are responses to increasingly strict safety standards demanded by insurance companies.

Rigorous social codes have also emerged as moral commentary on people's handling of their own landscapes. This commentary is nowhere more intricately entwined with official codes than in the suburban front lawn. A plethora of ordinances regulate front lawns in North America. While the lawn is a symbol of home ownership, of property and all the freedoms and powers that come with it, it is also a site for acute compliance rather than freedom.

The architects Diller + Scofidio's exhibit, *Docket*, illuminates how these ordinances sustain a level of absurd conformity in the life of American suburbs.[7] *Docket* presents photographs of suburban front yards and transcripts taken from a series of court cases concerning lawn maintenance. Recalling the circus-like format of the television show *Judge Judy*, Diller + Scofidio pair excerpts from actual testimonies of plaintiffs and defendants, with the judge's eventual ruling. Accompanying the text are photographs that document the subtle yet disquieting divisions between neighbor's lawns. These divisions of property are made apparent only by slight changes in the color of green, the texture of blades of grass, or different mowing patterns—small marks of difference in a landscape of conformity.

Docket's case of the City of Williamsport versus Sobocinski for failure to cut grass illustrates how little freedom we have as designers of our own front lawns. Sobocinski did not mow his lawn regularly and allowed weeds to grow. When taken to court Sobocinski defended his lawn claiming that the city's weed ordinance was an invalid exercise of police power. He also claimed that the city's ordinance was vague because weeds were defined as something unwanted. He wanted and enjoyed the plants growing in his yard. The court dismissed his defense because the judge found that "individual vegetal preferences were hardly relevant to the interpretation and enforcement of the ordinance."[8] Both comedy and tragedy, *Docket* reveals how the practices of surveillance and forced compliance limit authorship at the heart of our existence, the home.

Through questionnaires, interviews, meetings and work-shops, the general public also gets to be designers. There are several reasons for this. Landscapes, such as parks, are often used by the public or by special groups of people, such as children. Many landscape architects argue that people using these landscapes should be participants in the design process. It is felt that if people vote or work to consensus on the design of a landscape, then the result will be more democratic, reflecting more views and values than a singular designer could possibly envision. Public involvement helps designers who wish to avoid the individualistic stamp of Kant's rule-defying artists.

Historically, a major benefit of this public involvement was that it enabled poor and disenfranchised people to have a say in the design of spaces that shaped the fabric of their daily lives—parks, playgrounds, residential courtyards, and so forth. During the 1960s and 1970s public participation flourished, but by the 1990s, it became dominated by special interest groups and design review boards. These groups were often comprised of landowners and business people seeking to enhance their property values and limit liability risks. Given the shift from social integration to economic conservation, the impetus for equity in design was largely eclipsed.

Nonetheless, specific tools were developed to integrate the public as designers. One such tool is the questionnaire. Comprised of multiple-choice questions or a ranking system, questionnaires are often employed to determine the content and style of landscapes. Oregon respondents to a park questionnaire could choose from pathway types, plant varieties, dog poop bags, off-leash areas, open grassy areas, sports fields, and/or playgrounds. Questionnaires efficiently integrate many perspectives into the design of one landscape. As a method for discerning what elements people want to use in a landscape it is paramount. However, as a method of design—literally the form and composition of a work—will it produce landscapes that people expect more than what they want? Can a questionnaire produce a great work such as Central Park or an unexpected one, like Blue Stick Garden?

From Russia with Love

Vitaly Komar and Alexander Melamid, émigrés from the former Soviet Union, used questionnaires to create America's most and least wanted paintings. They asked people about specific features, such as color, content, and theme. Based on the answers they received, they produced two paintings, *America's Most Wanted* and *America's Most Unwanted*.[9] *America's Most Wanted* painting is about the size of the front of a dishwasher, features a naturalistic landscape with trees and a tranquil blue lake, distant mountains, and blue sky. George Washington and a group of hikers, and deer are also contained in the painting. *America's Most Unwanted* is a much smaller painting with an abstract composition of primarily orange, pink, and yellow shards.

Komar and Melamid polled people in other countries, including Iceland, Denmark, Turkey, China, Ukraine, Russia, France, and Kenya, and they painted a *Most Wanted* and a *Most Unwanted* painting based on each country's answers. Looking at the various *Most Wanted* paintings derived from this international questionnaire, the predominance of naturalistic looking landscapes with blue lakes and skies is striking.

But does this process actually produce paintings people want? Philosopher Arthur Danto thinks that the *Most Wanted*

Figure 1.1 Komar and Melamid, *America's Most Wanted* (photo credit: D. James Dee, © Komar and Melamid, Courtesy Ronald Feldman Fine Arts, New York)

paintings are paintings that nobody wants.[10] The paintings themselves are unexceptional, and the questionnaire format leads to strange meetings of historical and contemporary figures, and plants that bloom simultaneously in spring and fall. Danto argues that the preference for naturalistic landscapes reflects what people expect to see in paintings—landscapes. Even the fact that people in Kenya preferred the flooded valley of a Luminist work signals the role that calendar art has played in introducing non-Westerners to what conventional painting should look like.

Komar and Melamid went on to collaborate with elephants, beavers, and termites, but their approach to painting with the general public raises important questions about the role of artists in society and artistic methods. For example, questionnaires have a limited field of selection, and suggestions outside the statistically normal range of responses are discounted.

Does design by questionnaire give us the least objectionable rather than the most wanted?

The application of this method in the design of landscapes will also produce nothing more than what we expect. As Dewey points out, if we only want landscapes that fulfill what we expect they should look like, then we prevent growth. So how do we encourage people to design boldly, and what will we discover if we allow for experimentation and innovation?

Tilbury's Wandering Horses and Ponies

The London art collaborative, muf, had this question in mind in 2003 when they were selected to design a community garden for a social housing complex in Tilbury, England.[11] The complex, Broadway Estate, was created in the 1970s. Like many shared housing developments from this era, it is characterized by tall uniform towers that dwarf an expansive, empty common space, only punctuated by old playground equipment and parking.

Speaking with the residents, muf found that people living in Broadway Estate felt alienated from the rest of Tilbury and from themselves. This was exacerbated by a lack of outdoor social spaces that estate residents or other residents of Tilbury would want to use. City representatives identified a community garden as a good solution to the problem. But as muf notes, the call for professionals to design this garden was significant for what it did not mention.

During muf's visit to the Broadway Estate site and through 12 months of interactions with residents, they discovered that the people of Broadway Estate shared a very special relationship with the land and its inhabitants—one that was being restricted by increasingly oppressive land use regulations.

Recalling Surrealists' deambulations, where artists walked the city to uncover the unconscious landscapes that remained immune to modern transformation, muf discovered the wandering horses and ponies of Tilbury.

For centuries, the landscape of Tilbury had been home to nomadic gypsies who relied on horses to pull caravans. As the gypsies modernized their means of transportation, their horses and ponies were left to roam unencumbered by the spatial logic of post-horse Tilbury. By the end of the twentieth century, roaming ponies and horses were still features of Tilbury, but they were increasingly in conflict with the development of highways, ditches, and green commons. Ironically, the animals, which were valued as part of the landscape, were increasingly trespassers upon it. People complained of their excursions into vegetable patches, and they also feared for their safety and survival.

In their discussions with Broadway Estate residents, muf recognized the animals' acute presence in the minds of the residents, and knew it was key to the design. In response, muf's design was not a community garden at all, but three zones: a play area for young children that is within sight of the community house, an athletic field that is flanked by steps that create an amphitheater, and an arena for the horses. To celebrate the new landscape, muf designed a performance ritual to receive the horses and ponies at the estate. Working with local children they created life size effigies of ponies and horses. On inauguration day, the children dressed in their pony costumes and followed in procession behind real horses across the marshland, into the town, and to the new arena of Broadway Estate.

According to muf, this event symbolically and literally made a space within the landscape for what was otherwise "strategically suppressed."[12] Today the horse arena is well used by estate horse riders and other riders from Tilbury. This project demonstrates that multiple designers can be brought together to create a landscape that is wanted, but perhaps not expected. While it could be argued that the horses and ponies have now been contained by our progressively compartmentalized lives, their presence as part of Broadway Estate offers direct experiences with animals that are often inaccessible to people living in shared housing complexes.

NATURE AS DESIGNER
The Forgotten Garden that Never Was

The question of who designs landscapes is further complicated in a way that other practices, such painting or quilting, are not. Landscapes often contain and are subject to non-human factors that greatly influence their character over time. Natural processes, such as soil erosion and growing plants, can significantly shape landscapes. Paintings are subject to natural forces too, but these are incidental (unless they destroy the painting). Natural forces in landscapes are not incidental. They are often part of the landscape.

Consider Rottenrow Garden in Glasgow. The site was formerly occupied by an immense and rambling building, the Glasgow Royal Maternity Hospital, dating back to the nineteenth century. Despite being a world-renowned gynecology center, the facility was deemed inadequate by twenty-first century standards. In 2001, the city built a new hospital elsewhere and sold the structure to the University of Strathclyde. The University decided to remove the building and retained the landscape architecture firm Gross Max to design a temporary garden while it planned how to best use the property for a new building.

While the hospital was dismantled, the space of the Rottenrow Garden was literally created. As the rubble was gradually removed people noticed that this site had a very nice south-facing slope that looked over the skyline of the city and created breathing room within the dense urban fabric of Glasgow. Gross Max reused stone from the building to create retaining walls that terraced the garden. They also retained the ornate hospital entrance as an entry point into the site. New stairways and ramps were added to allow people to climb the slope.

Gross Max planted the terraced garden with snowdrops (the symbol of the hospital), but also with ample amounts of vigorous plants, such as self-clinging vines, pioneer specie trees, and hardy grasses. The shear explosion of biomass during Scotland's short growing season rapidly covered the site. In this way, the natural force of plant growth was exploited

Figure 1.2 Gross Max, Rottenrow Garden (photo credit: Gross Max)

as part of the designed landscape. Only three years later the garden's plants and old walls had a patina that led many to believe that it had been there much longer. The stairways, sculptures, and water features were obviously new and human-made, but the groves of multi-stemmed birch trees, waving clumps of grass, and Virginia creeper that covered the site rendered it a forgotten garden that never was.

Rottenrow Garden soon became tremendously popular among students and other city residents. Gross Max's lead designer, Bridget Baines, remarked if you want people to take your landscape as a given, plant fast-growing trees and grasses, and people will fight to save them.[13] The approach worked. Rottenrow Garden was initially a temporary solution, but the University eventually abandoned its plans for a new building and kept the garden.

The Nature of Myths

When our perception of time is altered by a landscape this can have the two-fold effect of making it appear older than it actually is, while also erasing the signs of human intervention that made it possible. For example, people visiting New York City often think that Central Park was just there, and the city was built up around it, with designers adding buildings, roads, fountains, and paths along the way. They are unaware of the massive physical transformations made to the 341 hectares of swamp land and rock outcrop in the nineteenth century. These transformations involved the importation of four million cubic meters of dirt for fill and hill creation, rock blasting that required 350 metric tons of gunpowder, planting 270,000 trees and shrubs, and tragically, the removal of one of Manhattan's first African American villages, Seneca, which was home to 1600 people.[14]

In this way, landscapes can be designed to look like natural givens—what has always been there. These landscapes serve as myths about humans and nature. A myth can be a story or set of ideas that represents or elaborates a belief, regardless if it is the truth, and sometimes it is deliberately a false belief or account. This is what the semiotician Roland Barthes thought. In his satirical accounts of everyday objects from food to advertising to soap, he revealed that they do not intrinsically harbor specific meaning, rather they elaborate contemporary myths. *Foamy* detergents, for example, cleverly convey the myth that the "liquid fire" of detergents has no harmful effects, and can even be good for the skin. "What matters is the art of having disguised the abrasive function of the detergent under the delicious image of a substance at once deep and airy which can govern the molecular order of material without damaging it."[15] By unmasking the myth behind things, Barthes sought to reveal how they are transformed into something that is considered universal or natural.

There are certain myths that landscapes are uniquely qualified to portray. The notion that people in pre-industrial societies lived in concert with nature and only moderately changed their environment is a common landscape myth in Western culture. This is likely the appeal of the *Most Wanted* paintings. A whopping 66 percent of the people questioned called for paintings depicting outdoor scenes that contained people in "natural settings."[16] Only 3 percent of Americans wanted a painting of a city. As a result, the *Most Wanted* paintings feature people in landscapes that are only moderately shaped by humans. These are scenes of peasants tending sparse patches of vegetation, children playing at the edges of wooded groves, or bare-breasted women caring for babies in fields.

The *Most Wanted* paintings reproduce the Romantic myth that landscapes should look as if they were shaped by natural processes more than human ones. This myth was exposed by Jean-Jacques Rousseau's character Saint-Preux in *Julie, ou la Nouvelle Heloise* (1761). Visiting the estate of his former lover, Julie, and her husband Wolmar, he is perplexed by their newly designed landscape. Chiefly, he is struck by the lack of signs of human intervention compared with other gardens. Walking through their new garden he remarks, "considering all this, I found it rather strange that they should take such pains to hide from themselves those they had taken; were it not better to have taken none at all."[17] Saint-Preux exclaims to Julie and her husband, "I see no human footsteps." "Exactly," replies Julie's husband, "it is because we have taken great pains to efface them."[18]

One interpretation suggests that Julie's landscape is redesigned to represent an original state of nature as a means of restoring her own virtue; a reordering of origins. It takes her back to a time before Saint-Preux was her lover. In the end it neither fools Saint-Preux nor satisfies Julie. The past is only redeemed by her death.

But why are many non-fiction landscapes designed to erase human intervention? What loss are they seeking to redress? These are important questions because in decoding what myths landscapes represent, we can better understand what landscapes are.

Two

THE "LANDSCAPE IDEA"
The Past Made Present

To represent is to stand for something else. For centuries landscapes have represented humans living in harmony with nature. During Rousseau's time the European imagination was captured by the notion of North America as an untouched specimen of raw nature; a veritable wild garden replete with local inhabitants who lived in harmony within its largesses. According to historian Leo Marx, it was conceived as "a place apart, secluded from the world—a peaceful, lovely place, classless, bountiful pasture."[1]

Gardens and sacred landscapes featured frequently in the histories of numerous religions as emblems for human genesis. Yet, seemingly clipped from the pages of history, here was a past that was present. This quality of pastness represented by North America led to intense speculation on human origins and our relationship with nature. It also fulfilled an idea about landscapes, which according to geographer Denis Cosgrove, has been in the making since the Renaissance. Cosgrove calls this the "landscape idea," a representation of collective life in nature, which was conceived in response to social and economic changes in people's relationship to land.[2]

When capitalist economies and industrial practices developed in Northern Europe, and eventually in North America, the notion of land as the bearer of sustenance was supplanted with land as property. This altered our relationship with land from appreciating its productive capacities to support life and structure society to envisioning it as simply another commodity for acquisition along with jewels, cars, and clothing. Yet, according to Cosgrove, landscapes have a special power among these possessions. They can provide us with potent spatial and sensorial experiences, such as seasonal changes, that recall versions of our old relationship with land as sustenance.

In the formation of the United States the landscape idea represented the country's social, political, and moral bearings. For example, Thomas Jefferson viewed working the land as the only moral and egalitarian way to make money in his new country. With his frequently quoted charge that "those who labor in the earth are the chosen people of God,"[3] he conferred upon the farmer a level of moral integrity and earnestness that could never be attained by a factory worker or accountant.

Stuck in Reverse

The landscape idea poses problems for what contemporary landscapes can represent. Landscapes are synthetic spaces where our perception of time has been altered, but the landscape idea inevitably puts this perception in reverse. It denotes a sense of loss—lost nature, lost community. This is why the landscape idea is rarely a focus of what is called modern art. If landscapes can only represent the past, how can they express the modern drive for progress?

At the end of the nineteenth century, when the profession

of landscape architecture was just beginning, people were feeling the full weight of modern civilization—its institutions, systems of organization, modes of production and its unrequited desire for progress. As Karl Marx and Friedrich Engels predicted, "all that is solid melts into air, all that is holy is profaned, and man is at last compelled to face with sober senses his real conditions of life, and his relations with his kind."[4]

These "real" conditions and relationships troubled Olmsted, as well. Olmsted was deeply concerned with the social alienation among people living in North America's growing industrial cities. He was disturbed that people never greeted one another on the street or even looked each other in the eye. With Calvert Vaux, he designed urban parks as bucolic spaces with meadows, lakes, winding paths, and shady groves. He believed these landscapes—drawn from the New England countryside of his childhood as well as the eighteenth-century English Landscape tradition—would not only promote people's mental and physical health, but encourage the tightly knit social fabric of rural communities.[5] Thus, the profession of landscape architecture was often assigned the role in modern society of designing landscapes that revived the past, where people lived in harmony with each other and with nature.

Another problem with the landscape idea is that it is not true. It is more of an ideal than an idea. In actuality, environmental devastation, widespread poverty, and destitution characterized many peoples' lives in pre-capitalist societies. While the industrial revolution started our warming of the planet, as early as the fifteenth century, the quest to build ships in Europe—for trade as well as war—depleted the continent of prime timber, which in turn increased flooding of urban areas, damaged crops, and reduced the amounts of wild game for hunting.

When Europeans discovered America, many of its inhabitants had already dramatically shaped the land with massive effigy mounds and artificial mountains, such as Monk's Mound in Illinois (800–1350), and extensive roadway systems, such as the remarkably straight roads made by the Anasazi (900–1150). As Europeans began farming North America they faced the vagaries of extreme weather (such as droughts), pest infestation, resource depletion, and labor shortages. We also know that their farming practices were often wasteful, and did not contribute to sustaining a collective life with nature. Subsequently, the average life expectancy was thirty-eight years old, half the years estimated today.

So why the unrequited desire for historical fantasy in the form of the landscape idea, why do we want landscapes to represent a past that is false? Because the landscape idea enables us to recast our origins—much in the way Rousseau's Julie attempted to recast her own history. Unquestionably, this recasting of origins is nowhere more evident than in touristic landscapes.

IDEOLOGY
Landscapes with a Past

In the *Necessity for Ruins*, Jackson was disturbed by living history environments created for tourists. These environments, such as Old Town Albuquerque and Colonial Williamsburg, stressed the consumable images and objects of the past rather than the lessons to be learned from it. Describing our quest to consume them in the form of token objects, evidentiary photographs, and period dress; Jackson writes, "why do people derive pleasure and even inspiration from the deliberate re-building or invention of historical environments," particularly when they erase the sequence of political events that make our historical existence possible?[6] He was perplexed by the new historic landscapes that were replacing historical monuments. According to Jackson an historical monument serves to remind us of our obligations, our social contract with the future that is fortified by what we have learned from the past.

For example, consider the monument dedicated to Abraham Lincoln in Washington D.C.. This neoclassical monument not only contains a larger-than-life sculpture of Lincoln, but it is inscribed with proclamations by Lincoln, such as the Gettysburg Address. Since 1922 it has accommodated pivotal events, such as Dr. Martin Luther King's speech, "I Have a Dream," and political rallies concerning civil rights. It is a reminder of how we should conduct ourselves and provides a place where this can be reaffirmed for future generations. It's not an experiential immersion into the past with Abe.

In contrast, an historic landscape "suggests that the past is a remote, ill-defined period or environment when a kind of golden age prevailed, when society had an innocence and a simplicity that we have since lost."[7] Historic landscapes for tourism are not simply commercial enterprises, but ideological ones that reshape history for our own purposes. They reconstruct our origins in a way that both defines and validates our present culture. We seek them to see ourselves as part of an "original design" and for Jackson this is why we have a *necessity* for ruins. We must abandon main street so that we can recreate it and correct history, reformulate it so that "we are charmed into a state of innocence and become part of the environment."[8]

Landscape theorist Dean MacCannell posits that postmodern people are proverbial tourists, seeking to imbibe the histories of other times and/or cultures as part of who they are.[9] He thinks people don't want the real, rather a themed, sanitized rendition of the real that they can experience and consume. And our desire for these renditions does not stop with amusement parks or historic old towns, rather it constitutes a lifestyle, formulating a sense of not only personal identity, but home and community identity.

Naturalizing Landscapes

But what's wrong with using history to garner a sense of collective identity? The past thirty years have witnessed the development of extensive historic zoning laws and preservation regulations that have saved important buildings and landscapes throughout the world. Yet, what if these seemingly good practices actually hinder the very aims that a history claims?

This is what geographers Nancy Duncan and James Duncan found in their study of Bedford, New York.[10] Bedford's historical development as a colonial farming settlement dates back to the seventeenth century, and today it perpetuates this image through historic and nature preservation regulations. For example, large-lot zoning for 4-acre home sites has been enforced to limit density that might be associated with a city. Likewise, Bedford's tree preservation code has been implemented to maintain the look of an agrarian landscape, rather than fulfilling a specific ecological role.

Since Jefferson's time colonial farming communities in the United States have represented the idea of a morally superior, classless, and egalitarian society. In Leo Marx's interpretation of Jefferson's America, "the true American is the ploughman, whose values are derived from his relations to the land, not from 'artificial rules.' "[11] However, the Duncans found that the historical image maintained by Bedford actually limits it ability to fulfill these ideals.

Using extensive interviews, town-wide surveys, textual studies of local papers, and an analysis of the landscape itself, the Duncans found that Bedford's current perpetuation of itself as the real rendition of an agrarian settlement is inaccurate because its residents don't really work the land of Bedford. In fact, the Duncans reveal that Bedford's land is actually maintained by Latino workers who must live elsewhere. The town's historic zoning and environmental restrictions have made Bedford unaffordable to working class people. As a result, the people who Bedford homeowners depend on for the care of their children and elderly, cleaning and repair of their houses, and maintenance of their lawns and gardens are excluded.

For the Duncans, Bedford's historic and nature preservation regulations are part of residents' desire to keep their landscape untainted by the labor that maintains it. Laborers are welcomed in Bedford in their capacity as service workers, but not as neighbors.[12] Without a doubt, Bedford represents a former farming community, but it is not morally superior, classless, nor egalitarian. Instead, it uses the moral edification of a traditional farming community to establish and maintain class boundaries, ultimately restricting who can afford to live there in a seemingly natural state of affairs.

So how can landscapes represent the past without using it to validate the present? How can historic artifacts be preserved, while allowing for present needs?

Rest Stop

In his design of numerous historic sites in France, landscape architect Bernard Lassus explores the relationship between the imaginary elements of the past and real ones in a way that heightens our awareness of their distinction. Lassus's design for a motorway "Rest Stop" at Nîmes-Caissargues, France is an example. This region of France is steeped in history. The nearby city of Nîmes claims artifacts such as the aqueduct Pont du Gard, Nîmes amphitheater, and Tour Magne that are testimonies to Roman engineering virtuosity. However Lassus does not design Rest Stop as a rendition of the past; making this roadside amenity a seamless extension of the region's history. Instead, Lassus juxtaposes the present with the past, and asks us to consider their difference.

This difference is heightened by the changes in velocity from car to foot, as pathways at Rest Stop guide the walking motorist through a circuit of belvederes and lookouts that provide views to the Tour Magne and other features in the region. During the first century, the Tour Magne was the highest tower along Nîmes's ancient defense walls. Visible from a great distance, it marked the presence of the town and the sanctuary of a spring at the foot of the hill. This is an important view from Rest Stop, but the belvedere structures do not recreate the historic Tour Magne. Instead, these viewing structures are undeniably current to our own times—made from metal mesh that traces the outline of the historic structure in a graphic silhouette. Located on high points in this ancient terrain, these belvederes each contain a maquette of the Tour Magne, which is the tactile counterpoint to the real tower that can be seen from that point in space. Touching the maquette—the imaginary Tour Magne—and viewing the real one, the imaginative present is connected, but distinct, from the historic edifice.

In addition to the circuit of views from the belvederes, the Nîmes-Caissargues Rest Stop also has washrooms, a small

Figure 2.1 Bernard Lassus, Caissargues Rest Stop Belvedere (photo credit: Atelier Bernard Lassus)

museum, and it accommodates parking for trucks and cars. These are organized around a 700 meter long avenue space bound by rows of trees on each side. This type of avenue space was the great garden invention of the seventeenth century. During the Baroque period illusionary space was not only the province of mathematics and painting, but it was actualized by Le Nôtre in his garden designs, especially in his avenue spaces.

Capturing the dynamic between perspective view and point of view, long avenue spaces in Le Nôtre's gardens created a mathematically defined nature that played against the movement of the body. For example, at Vaux-le-Vicomte he manipulated the slope and width of the main axis so that garden features, such as the statue of Hercules, appear further as you get closer to them. Also, traveling along the main north–south axis, the largest element in the garden, the Grand Canal, can

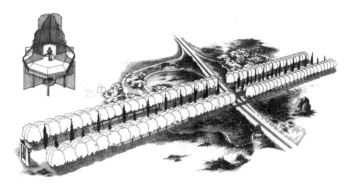

Figure 2.2 Bernard Lassus, Caissargues Rest Stop (photo credit: Atelier Bernard Lassus)

be heard, but it is impossible to see until you are only a few meters away from it.[13]

At Rest Stop, Lassus juxtaposes this avenue space from French garden history with the reality of the present by crossing the autoroute with it.[14] Wider and lined with trees, the scale of this avenue dwarfs the slender lines of the motorway. Although it is literally bisected by the motorway, the spatial boundaries of the avenue continues over it, sloping towards the view of Nîmes. Here, the present is not blurred with the past, rather these realities are represented to us in all their poignant contradictions. Walking this landscape, the onward rush of the vehicles contrasts with the quiet illusionary space of the avenue; colliding two preeminent landscape types of the seventeenth and twentieth centuries—the majestic space of the avenue and that of the open road.

PICTORIALIZING NATURE
Keeping up Appearances
Writers like Rousseau, poets, and painters in the English school of landscape painting helped define the visual attributes

of the landscape idea. In Medieval and early Renaissance paintings, landscapes only served as backgrounds to religious scenes or portraitures, but by the seventeenth century, landscapes themselves emerged as central subjects of the painted canvass. Painters like Claude Lorrain gave us representations where people figured only as small brush strokes upon the scene. Later English painters, such as John Constable, refined the tradition by creating scenes where people shared the canvass with the landscape. Similar to the *Most Wanted* series, the landscape idea contained people who were at once beholden to and in harmony with their environment of blue lakes and skies, attractive animals, and plentiful vegetal life.

According to landscape architect Gina Crandell, from this point onward a narrow set of conventions or what she calls "pictorializing practices" were employed.[15] These practices defined how to represent nature in painting and landscapes. They dictated the content of paintings, such as distant mountains, large deciduous trees, rolling grass hills, and flooded valleys; and they also defined specific compositional techniques like curved lines, rough textures, deep shadows, and filtered sunlight.

These conventions forged in landscape painting directly informed the design of physical landscapes. Like their painted counterparts, landscapes designed in this tradition contained large trees, rolling hills, and flooded valleys. They gave us the image of what nature should look like, but also landscapes, impoverishing both. For example, many people think that nature has curved or crooked lines, and that straight lines, geometric forms, and symmetry are not natural. Yet, there are straight branches, symmetries in snow flakes, and while the moon is not a perfect sphere, it would be disconcerting to look up one evening to a glowing amoebic form in the sky. Likewise, our bodies have bilateral symmetries.

Many misconceptions concerning the look of nature can be traced back to writings about landscapes that sought to imitate nature. Consider again Walpole's description of William Kent's landscape designs.

> Having routed *professed* art, the modern gardener exerts his talents to conceal his art, Kent, like other reformers, knew not how to stop at the just limits. He had followed nature, and imitated her so happily, that he began to think all her works were equally proper for imitation. In Kensington Garden he planted dead trees, to give a greater air of truth to the scene— but he was soon laughed out of this excess. His ruling principle was, that *nature abhors a straight line*. His mimics, for every genius has his apes, seemed to think that she could love nothing but what was crooked.[16]

Walpole's writing about landscapes charted the course for what we think landscapes should look like, but nature as well. In response, contemporary landscape architects have been designing parks and gardens that challenge the pictorial practices forged in the eighteenth century. Many of their landscapes follow a strict geometry of shapes and straight lines, or a quirky series of zigzag forms. These obviously human-made shapes and patterns announce to people that this landscape is not the chance results of natural processes, or pictorializing practices.

Barrier Park

Barrier Park in East London is characterized by straight walks, sharp angled cuts into the land, and linear compositions of plants. These major features of the park take their clue from the site's previous industrial use. The park occupies a former chemical and dye works, armaments factory, and tarmac plant. These land uses have marked the site with deep linear cuts and right-angled alignments; moves once governed by expediency and logistics that are now but abstractions.

Walking from the tube station to this park is a surreal journey; a dizzying collage of abandoned industrial relics, derelict buildings, moving cranes, highways, interspersed with small scale agricultural uses. For example, in the center of the highway's clover-leaf ramp—what Lewis Mumford called America's national flower—a horse looks up with a blank stare as cars swirl around him in the chute-like space created by the egress lane.

The entrance to the park is marked by a plaza with thirty-two water jets that project luminescent garlands of water into

Figure 2.3 Alain Provost, Barrier Park (photo credit: Susan Herrington)

the air. They are the source of amusement for several children who try to stop the flow with great exuberance. The designer of the park, landscape architect Alain Provost, uses the former dock land topography as the park's central organizing feature. Provost retraces the 5 meter deep former dry dock—utilized when the land was an industrial site—as a sunken garden.

The garden's steep sides are improbably planted with hedges that seem to defy gravity. The base of this hollowed space contains paths and rows of perennial plants alternating with evergreen hedges. The linear persistence of the rows is animated by the lively movement of the perennial plants in the wind, which contrasts with the motionless evergreen hedges that have been trimmed in the form of waves. Above, a series of paths border the edges and cross over this sunken garden orienting you to a view of the River Thames and the flood control structures, which keep the city dry. At the water's edge a tall pavilion, which relates to the scale of the River and the large sunken garden, provides shade. An adjacent field is hosting a game of frisbee.

The formal qualities of the park—its shapes and forms— tell me that this landscape is a human designed space. It also rejects the tabula rasa approach of landscape as the image of ideal nature because it takes advantage of the existing industrial topography as a central feature of the park. Provost had no desire to pictorialize nature here, to design a park as if it was the sole result of natural processes. Instead, his design embraces both its past human uses and the fact that it is shaped again by humans.

On this particular visit a bus pulls up to the entry and a large group of elderly women descend upon the park. These were the same women seen on a visit to a more traditional English garden, Wisley. Undaunted by the park's strikingly bold design—its straight lines, its sleek architectural features, the funky hedge that grows from the steep walls of the sunken garden—they are immediately drawn to the park. They engage in the same activities observed at Wisley—identifying plants, discussing their experiences with certain plants versus others. Of course, this leads to discussions about people they know and places they've traveled. This is an important social function of gardens, particularly for elderly people, and it's good to see them enjoying themselves.

Wildlife is also unencumbered by the design of the landscape. Numerous bird species have been spotted using the park, including sparrow hawks, kestrels, and peregrines. Grey herons feed along the shore, and teal and shelduck are commonly spotted. Even the architectonic hedges that line the walls of the sunken garden are suddenly alive with movement as birds who have made nests in their planted walls take flight.

WHAT'S WORTH REPRESENTING
Real versus Ideal Landscapes

But what's wrong with creating landscapes that conform to a very narrow set of conventions of what nature looks like? Perhaps we need these conventional representations of nature? Some environmental psychologists say yes. By methodically exposing people to images of landscapes that pictorialize nature they have found that these landscape scenes are beneficial to our mental states. They make us feel better because we can imagine that our landscapes have no shopping malls, crowded highways, drive-by shootings, and rider lawn mowers. In a North American context, these representations can have great significance for people of non-native ancestry. It relieves them of technological and pioneer guilt by recalling the pre-European settlement landscape of North America. This was before it was drained of over 50 percent of its wetlands, virtually erased of its local inhabitants, and extensively polluted.

But don't we all want to be fooled sometimes, alleviated from the angst of the present by revisiting a golden past in harmony with nature?

Landscapes designed to pictorialize nature may not only distort what we think nature looks like, but also how it works. This distortion can disconnect us from real nature. In our fight for fantasy, the landscape architect Robert L. Thayer maintains that we have a highly dichotomized—if not schizophrenic—understanding of the world and our place in it. For Thayer, we have landscapes that pictorialize nature as an ideal image and landscapes that actualize the real mechanism of everyday life—two simultaneously lived worlds.[17]

The ideal landscape looks like the perfect type of landscape we would like to live in. For example, I may like the look of farmland, the gently rolling hills of grain and the cows lying about the grassy slopes. Since I was a child I've seen paintings and drawings in books that impart this perfect type of landscape image. I write "perfect type of landscape" because physically living in an ideal landscape may contradict this ideal. I may move next to a farm to get closer to this ideal, but I soon realize that farmers spray their fields with pesticide, they get up at five in the morning to operate noisy machinery, and cow manure doesn't smell that great and attracts flies the size of golf balls. Nonetheless, ideal landscapes direct our choice of homes, the types of recreational activities we enjoy, and where we vacation and seek entertainment. They also contain technologies that we deem good like high-tech bicycles, tomatoes all year long, and air conditioning on hot days.

However, these good technologies are often linked to real landscapes and technologies we deem bad.

Real landscapes represent the way we know the world actually works. They direct our choice of jobs, schools, and what we can actually afford. Real landscapes are seemingly directed by forces that lie beyond our individual control, such as the real estate market. They also contain large infrastructure projects like highways and sewage treatment plants that we consider bad and want to keep separate from our ideal landscapes. According to Thayer, these two distinct worlds and our desire to keep them separate lie at the crux of current environmental problems.

What landscapes are designed to represent is critical because landscapes designed in the twentieth century have played a significant role in camouflaging Thayer's real landscapes, while simultaneously elaborating ideal ones. The power lines that cut through a state forest are carefully screened with plantings so that visitors driving through the park can't see them. An exhausted limestone quarry is made into an ornamental garden with the importation of thousands of cubic meters of topsoil, trees, shrubs, and winding paths to make me forget it was a quarry.

If landscapes are designed to look like they are a product of solely natural processes, they hide the very human intervention that makes them possible. They lobotomize the evidence of our existence in the world, both the good and the bad repercussions of it. So why not broaden the scope of what landscapes can represent? Why not design landscapes in ways that communicate ideas about how nature really works—as a process—or how most of our landscapes are supported by an intricate network of human and biophysical processes?

Real Ideal Landscapes

For example, infrastructure landscapes, once screened from the public, have been transformed so that their functional operations can be seen and interpreted by people. Many of these landscapes challenge "real world" landscapes that we consider disagreeable and want to keep separate from our ideal landscapes. They also question the single function capacity of most infrastructure landscapes by integrating other uses.

When completed in 2010, the Brightwater Wastewater Treatment Facility will process water from both King and Snohomish counties in Washington state in a landscape open to the public.[18] Most water treatment plants avoid being seen, heard, and smelled. However, this landscape reinvents a region's "bad" infrastructure as a place for education and enjoyment. The Brightwater landscape introduces a system of canals and wetlands that provide tertiary treatment of wastewater and this process is made integral to visitors' experiences of the site. Designed by the landscape architecture office, Hargreaves Associates, one of the goals of this 46 hectare site is to foreground people's awareness of how they are connected to a real landscape. Thus, the treatment processes are not camouflaged from other traditional site functions. Instead, water cleansing areas overlap with pedestrian walks and bridges, and recreational and educational uses.

Still, all this "honest" human expression does not account for the underlying reasons why we want landscapes to pictorialize nature. A compelling reason may be the moral fortitude thought to be bestowed upon those who appreciate a landscape as nature. To deeply admire an environment or object as nature imparts to others that you are connected to something greater, something that has not been purposefully framed for presentation to humans.

Since nature, unlike art, has not been intentionally prepared for humans, it calls for a certain sympathy that requests you to privilege non-human achievements and concerns over human ones. This sympathy or sensitivity for the non-human has moral weight because it demonstrates that you are not concerned with simply human consequences, but a broader context of what is right and what is wrong—or does it? These are questions for the next chapter.

Are landscapes natural?

Three

INTERPRETATIONS OF NATURE
Landscapes and Nature

The landscape idea shapes not only the way landscapes look (the way they are designed, for example), but the way we see them *as*. For philosopher Ludwig Wittgenstein, "seeing as" is a change in perception made by the viewer and not the thing or space itself.[1] It is something that happens while we are simultaneously seeing and interpreting. Viewing the picture by psychologist Joseph Jastrow you may see the drawing as a duck or you may see it as a rabbit depending on what you want to see it as. "Seeing as" is to see Central Park as a landscape or, highlighting other senses, to smell a mixture of rose, sandalwood, vanilla and musk, as perfume. The landscape idea is so dominant and has such a particular set of scenic conventions that some people may have difficulty seeing landscapes that don't fit these conventions *as landscapes*.

Examples such as Barrier Park, which don't employ these scenic conventions, are landscapes, and they serve a wide variety of life and people enjoy them. Perhaps we can simply change our preference settings of landscape representations? Unfortunately it is more complicated than that. We know that landscapes often idealize past human life in nature—the "landscape idea"—and they are also subject to a long history

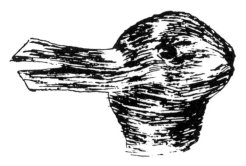

Figure 3.1 Duck–Rabbit (public domain)

of pictorializing nature. Thus, they are not only the optical consciousness of what we call nature, but the subconscious terrain of culture's relationship to nature. In other words many landscapes not only represent nature, but in doing so also demonstrate how we relate to it.

Because landscapes are so bound up in the relationship between nature and culture, I will shake out the arguments that attempt to know this relationship. Since the late 1940s, when doubt was cast upon modern industrialism, environmentalists, philosophers, and cultural theorists have been asking, how should we value and relate to nature? Three main camps have sought to answer this question and there are numerous splinter groups, as well as groups that attempt to coalesce the extremes. Their views carry fundamental differences, such as to what extent are human actions natural. However, they all share a deep suspicion of modernism—its institutions, organization, production, drive for progress, and its alienating conditions.

There are first wave conservationists who alerted us to the environmental devastation resulting from modern agricultural practices, such as overgrazing, and industrial practices, such as toxic waste dumping. This is commonly referred to as the

Aldo Leopold "land ethic," which holds that instead of plundering nature, we are duty bound to maintain healthy ecosystems for the benefit of the entire biotic community, humans included.[2]

Landscapes in the Leopold tradition serve as demonstrations of humans acting as good "stewards" of nature. These are conservation areas, scenic viewpoints, and trails where human use must be tempered with why these landscapes were conserved in the first place. While Leopold's work was directed towards large regional landscapes, his ideas influenced a range of landscapes scales. Contemporary defenders of Leopold's land ethic revere Leopold for challenging Cartesian conceptions of nature as an object that can be dissected and described by quantitative and hierarchal means. They claim humans are part of a complexly intertwined ecological community and we are accountable to maintaining its health.

Many second wave environmentalists deplore modernism like the first wave, but they tend to critique the first wave as ultimately anthropocentric and espousing an instrumental view of nature. To act as a steward of nature implies using nature for human betterment. Second wave environmentalists believe that we should hold an intrinsic value of nature. Our relationship with nature should honor nature for itself, and pleasure or benefits should not guide this relationship. However, they tend to agree that Cartesian subject/object relationships, which have largely governed human studies of nature, are the source of our environmental crisis. In fact, the Cartesian model is often viewed as a cunning accomplice in our exploitation of nature.

Ironically, both waves often embrace the fallacy that real nature tends towards an optimal balance, stability, or harmony. According to Darwin and contemporary science, nature is chaotic, complex, dangerous, and with no known optimal purpose. Both waves also view pre-modern societies as living in tune with nature, despite ample examples from anthropologists and archeologists that this was not always the case.

Getting Close to Nature

Some second wave environmentalists lend a peculiar twist to history with a preoccupation with origins. Mixing scientific and religious language to paint a mythic story of collective life in oneness with nature they rely heavily on the landscape idea as a source of inspiration. There is an emphasis placed on past traditions and mystic rituals that can bring us closer to nature. Philosopher Arne Naess, for example, claims that Deep Ecology is a movement that is grounded in both philosophy and religion. Elaborating further on this argument, Freya Mathews notes that Deep Ecology "is a matter of attitude, a spiritual matter, calling for an outright affirmation of nature, that maybe expressed in an infinite number of possible ways—from the private revering of a flower, through the devotional study of the natural sciences, to full-blown ritual celebrations in the style of the American Indians."[3]

Deep Ecology often identifies with the practices of "traditional or primal peoples" who are thought to sustain a natural order.[4] Unfortunately, it is difficult to pinpoint what these exact practices are because the landscape idea is not necessarily true. For example, the Native American settlement of Cahokia with its astrologically aligned wood henges and its sacred Monk's Mound was eventually abandoned by 1400. It's speculated that overgrazing and deforestation may have contributed to Cahokia's decline. But even if we wanted to believe in the landscape idea, how will it really connect contemporary people to nature? Philosopher Kate Soper notes that "it is not clear that by becoming more mystical or religious about nature one necessarily overcomes the damaging forms of separation or loss of concern" with nature.[5] Nonetheless, it is a powerful motivator for second wave agendas.

One such agenda conceived by second wave environmentalists, bioregionalists, is the demarcation of natural boundaries. They argue that modern society is alienated from nature and to become closer to nature we must submit to its laws. A proposal often made to attain this closeness to nature involves the identification and maintenance of ecological communities whose natural borders provide a template for political borders—borders by nature's law that should not be crossed. For example, one bioregionalist plan asserts that we should redraw the state borders of the United States to reflect natural boundaries rather than political ones.[6] These redrawn borders would trace law-abiding biophysical features such as rivers, mountain ranges, and forests. Moreover, people inhabiting these redrawn territories should remain in them.

There are scientific problems with this proposal. Ecological systems, even huge ones like the Mississippi River or tree populations which are commonly symbols of "rootedness," are continually adjusting their locations. To freeze life in a geographic region is to counter nature, its evolutionary processes of spatial diffusion through exchange and migration. Likewise to hold species' habitat in location as the optimal place for that species is not a law of nature. Evolutionary biologist and science historian, Stephen Jay Gould, notes that even plants we consider native cannot be deemed biologically best in any justifiable way . . . they are only the plants that happened to arrive first and be able to flourish (the evolutionary argument based on geography and history), while their capacity for flourishing only indicates a status as "better than" others available, not as optimal or globally "best suited."[7]

As a global outlook, there are serious social consequences with the bioregionalist proposal. A bioregionalist outlook is fine if you live in rural Oregon, but for people living in poverty, war, and oppression, staying within your pre-sumed "natural" borders is not an option, and hardly a humane one.

Me Nature, She Jane

Philosophers like Soper argue that second wave environmen-talists have continued to use women as symbols of nature—as a means to identify an "other" that needs to be interpreted and protected from abuse. The woman–nature connection has an extensive history in many cultures with women sym-bolizing various forms of nature, but it features heavily in second wave environmentalism. For example, the Earth First mantra exclaiming "No Compromise in the Defense of Mother Earth!"[8] inadvertently aligns women in a continual state of helplessness and exploitation. Soper contends that this type of "woman–nature coding," which has served to both legitimize and confine the role of women in society, ultimately excludes them from humanity and culture.[9] This critique highlights that we can't simply change the Earth First logo or call Leopold's stewards, "flight attendants." Rather, it begs a rethinking of feminist theory in regards to nature.

The third wave is comprised of cultural theorists who consider nature simply a construct. Cultural theorists point out that many of the symbols used to refer to nature are the products of race, gender, or class relations, rather than natural law. This correlates with Soper's point that the use of women as symbols for nature is more about power relations between men and women rather than anything we really know about nature.

They also have a problem with the intrinsic view of nature because to assign something as valuable—even when it is only valuable to itself—is a human activity that is dependent on a human evaluator to make this decision. Instead of being duty bound (like the conservationists) or subject to natural laws (like bioregionalists), cultural theorists argue that our relationship with nature is an invention created by society to sort out, classify, and maintain the status quo.

Nonetheless, humans are subject to natural forces, and do have natural needs for things like shelter, water, food, and love. If nature is simply an invented idea then how do we account for these needs? How can we understand the impact of landscapes on natural needs? Also, to reduce nature to the mental play of words might deprive us of sensorial pleasures gained from landscapes that contain natural elements.

Much like second wave environmentalist arguments, the cultural construct position is problematized by scientific evidence. There are natural consequences associated with managing ecosystems. Drinking contaminated water can kill you. Moreover, we are born into a world that is largely created without human intervention. Mountains are landscapes conditioned by our cultural practices of viewing them as landscapes, but humans are not accountable for their physical presence.

Similar to the environmentalists, cultural theorists hold deep reservations about Cartesian handlings of nature and often extend their critique to the entire Enlightenment project. However, the Cartesian subject/object position refers to a conceptual framework, and one that has been used for as much good as ill. As a framework it does not cause environmental damage—people's greed and ignorance do. Likewise, as a framework it does not allow us to literally separate our minds from our bodies or even necessarily our context. In fact, Cartesian thinking about nature can be driven by human needs and desires situated in a particular context.

Recall Dr. John Snow, who revealed through mapping the bastion of Cartesian thinking, how the Broad Street pump was the source of London's worst cholera outbreak in the nineteenth century. Snow's desire to solve the cholera problem by plotting the geographic locations of the deceased stemmed from witnessing the "terrible outbreak" and the death of more than three-quarters of the neighborhood's inhabitants.[10] Snow's ground breaking work in the nineteenth century compelled people to make ecological connections between the treatment of water and health. Only decades later, numerous parks, such as Frederick Law Olmsted's Back Bay Fens in Boston, were created to mitigate the relationship between people and polluted water.

Unfortunately, none of these arguments fully grasp our relationship with nature or how landscapes demonstrate this relationship. Nature in all three versions is held as a static system—a balanced community, a natural border, or a construct (although constructs are modified over time). This is odd given that one of the first most comprehensive and influential studies of nature, *The Origin of Species*, portrayed it as changing.

While Darwin's classic work was entitled *The Origin of Species*,[11] the idea of nature as origin is less important than the way Darwin's framework sets in motion the highly complex elaboration of the forces of nature, which continues to evolve. Theorist Elizabeth Grosz asserts that Charles Darwin's evolutionary theories share basic commonalities with culture in that they both highlight and privilege change and difference over time. For Grosz, Darwin has "outlined an ingenious temporal machine for production of the new" and this temporal machine is important because it provides a recourse to those who are oppressed.[12] Understanding nature as changing opens doors to people that "nature as origins" does not. For example, if Bedford's nature was grounded in maintaining change instead of maintaining its origins as a farming community, it might accommodate more people. Large lot zoning might be tempered with more affordable lot sizes and the earnest concern given the town's trees might extend to those who care for them.

Grosz is also emphatic that pleasure is a natural force. She stresses that pleasure is a biological and psychological component of human nature. It is also a subtle, but salient, feeling missing from many second wave interpretations of our relationship with nature. Their arguments for non-anthropocentric views of nature's intrinsic value reject not only human uses of nature, but human pleasures derived from it.

Nonetheless, human pleasure has shaped important pieces of environmental policy since the nineteenth century. Indeed, Romantics like Rousseau thought that an intrinsic value of nature was good for us, and it was this type of perspective that the park movement in the United States gave its purpose. For example, the United States Organic Act of 1916 was one of the earliest Congressional legislations to preserve nature for human enjoyment. This act mandated that national parks will

> conserve the scenery and the natural and historic objects and the wildlife therein and to provide for the enjoyment of the same in such manner and by such means as will leave them unimpaired for the enjoyment of future generations.[13]

Although this act will appear hopelessly outdated and anthropocentric to second wave environmentalists, how should nature and landscapes be valued?

Appreciating Nature

The answer to this question has been the subject of philosophical debates in regard to what type of nature is being appreciated—a pine cone or a forest—and how we should "see it as." For philosopher Malcolm Budd to appreciate the form of a snowflake (natural object), you must see its form as naturally produced.[14] Furthermore, nature should be appreciated for what it indicates.[15] I can marvel at the color, texture, and smell of jasmine, for example, but its presence also indicates that it is spring and this is equally important. According to Budd, nature "must not be the product of human skills or design or artifice" or even a work of God. Humans are nature but anything humans do or make is not nature.

This very succinct definition of seeing nature however, does not account for the complexity it implies, especially if we use Jackson's definition of landscapes. Consider the extensive tree planting in Northern Canada performed by youth every summer. This massive reforestation project, which began in the 1930s, is creating an extensive forest ecosystem. By 2030, when this forest has been left to "naturally" reproduce itself, will it be considered natural?

For most philosophers concerned with nature appreciation, landscapes cannot be considered nature because they have been designed either intentionally or unintentionally by humans. In fact, Budd writes that to appreciate a landscape as nature is "malfounded."[16] This would come to a great disappointment for people who set off on a hike through a managed forest or pull over at a scenic overlook to enjoy nature.

So where do we draw the line between nature and not nature, and do these dichotomies further fortify boundaries that should remain blurred? Landscapes are a product of this blurring where a teasing out of nature from non-nature is tricky. For example, there are natural features, such as the movement of the sun, that powerfully shape our experience with landscapes, but they are beyond human artifice and control. In contrast, many people find the gossamer pink hue across a setting sun beautiful, but the rose coloration is most likely caused by pollution.

But what's wrong with identifying human-designed landscapes as nature?

SEEING LANDSCAPES AS NATURE
Nature's Authority

What we deem nature asserts a powerful force over human life and relations as an inevitable given. If you are 160 centimeters tall, compared with someone who is 183 centimeters tall, you will have a "natural" disadvantage in placing suitcases in an overhead luggage compartment. Likewise, we are growing old, and even if we landscape ourselves—cut with liposuction and fill with botulinum—we will succumb to the inevitable forces of nature.

When landscapes are designed to look as if they are naturally created it entitles them to be inevitable, beyond our control. This is when landscapes function like an ideology—they naturalize cultural acts. For some geographers and historians landscapes do not simply signify or symbolize power relations, they are powerful agents in the practice of power.[17] This was certainly what the Duncans found in their analysis of Bedford.

The eighteenth-century English landscapes described thus far have been frequently assailed for mixing up who authored them—humans or nature. Inspired by descriptions of Chinese gardens and landscapes painted by Claude Lorrain, these landscapes were strikingly different from other gardens in Western history. They were purposefully designed to look as if they were authored by nature itself. Reflecting the landscape idea, their winding paths, moss covered ruins, clumps of trees, and rolling terrain confused the authorship of these works, so one might think the landscape had very little human intervention.

It's important to remember that these landscapes were created as part of Inclosure Acts in England. These acts enabled people to enclose land—literally with fences, hedgerows, and ditches—that was once commonly held. Once enclosed, the landowner hired tenant farmers who they paid a pittance to work it. Landscape designers were often hired to design gardens within the enclosed estate, and these gardens helped conceal the signs of enclosure—the fences, hedgerows, and toiling farmers.

It has been argued that the intentional conflation of landscapes and nature in the appreciation of these grand works was a means of "naturalizing" the power of their prosperous owners. Indeed, these landscapes were not only a testament that their owners possessed the informality that only the very rich could afford, but that this wealth was part of a natural order, a given. The landscape garden as a natural order, thus, contained a hierarchical world where the wealthy owned it and the poor toiled in it. And for the owners, "wasn't this only natural?"

The ideological use of nature in these landscapes includes the viewers as accessories to the way they see landscapes. In other words, the way the landscapes were designed enabled people to not only view the landscape as natural, but to view nature as a landscape. Recall Horace Walpole's description of William Kent who had "leaped the fence, and saw that all nature was a garden."[18] This facile movement from nature to landscape suggests that landscapes, although synthetic, can be appreciated as nature, and with all the moral fortitude that comes with it. One of the first critics to point this out was Mary Wollstonecraft. She argued that marveling at landscapes as nature appeared to denote a higher calling, an elevated level of moral integrity, in the viewer. But she also concluded that as a consequence of this higher calling to appreciate non-human nature—everything was revered in these gardens except humans.[19]

The Goodness of Nature

This leads to the second problem with thinking that landscapes are nature. There is a transference of good and righteousness assigned to those who claim to value them as such. Raymond Williams notes that since the eighteenth century two of the most persistent and powerful dimensions of nature are its "selective sense of goodness and innocence" and its ability to redeem a corrupt human society.[20] This supports Kant's idea that there is a moral capacity in appreciating nature. According to philosopher Ronald Moore, Kant thought "a direct interest, not just taste, in nature is always a mark of a good soul" and "at least indicative of moral feeling."[21] He not only thought that an appreciation of nature was a mark of goodness in a person, but that nature was essentially good. The random acts of nature were favored over the purposeful act of humans expressed in art. For Kant "if the natural object and the human-made object are, in all perceptible qualities, identical, then deeming the natural as natural would impute to its object some moral weight."[22]

Kant's sentiment about nature and goodness is echoed in other aesthetic treatises as well, such as Johann Georg Sulzer writing in *The General Theory of Fine Arts*. Regarding the work of landscape artists, Sulzer posits that "inanimate nature offers them an inexhaustible store of materials through which they can exercise a positive effect on men's character."[23] He even thought paintings of nature could give the viewing subject a moral fortitude unattainable by viewing works that did not depict nature.

Supporting this thesis by contrast is the Decadent Movement during the late nineteenth century. A central tenant of this movement was *not* to appreciate nature. Writers like Karl Huysmans and Oscar Wilde were bored with nature and all its moral edification. Huysmans' notorious character, des Esseintes, in *À Rebours* declares that the age of nature is past; it has finally exhausted the patience of all sensitive minds by the "sickening monotony" of its landscapes and skies.[24] Thus, des Esseintes travels the countryside in search of the artificial, the unnatural. Even in his perusal of flowers at a market full of "blossoms dazzling and cruel in their brilliance," he seeks "natural flowers imitating the false."[25] In this way, to deem objects as valuable for not being naturally produced was decadent.

The intrinsic and morally upright version of nature sits uncomfortably with what landscapes are. Landscapes are often highly instrumental and extrinsic, and not unabashedly good. More problematic, if landscapes are deemed natural and thus intrinsically valuable and good, this means they are not tinged by the expressions of culture—its politics, fashions, and ideologies. And what if landscapes are perceived as upholding nature's good intentions with humans as their faithful servants, but they are actually instrumental to a deadly political ideology?

Nature as Ideology

For some historians, it was precisely the apolitical dimension of early nature conservation landscapes and their unquestionable goodness that enabled them to be warped by Nazi ideology in Germany. In 1905, conservation groups stressed the scientific and historic implications of their work. Early nature protection and conservation work was initially independent of the political arena where it took place. However, by the 1930s the economic and physical environment of Germany was on the verge of collapse and the management of the nation's nature became an important vehicle to galvanize National Socialism.

Casting doubt on Germany's modern industrial project, proponents of National Socialism sought to preserve and perpetuate a pre-industrial landscape to legitimatize notions of racial superiority in connection with understanding nature. Garden historians, Gert Groening and Joachim Wolschke-Bulmahn, published some of the first descriptions of these ideological uses of nature in Germany.[26] For example, they found that the craze for native plants and the natural gardening movement during the 1930s was integral to defining the racist ideas of the Third Reich. A pseudo-history of traditional German folklore was exploited by the Nazis to demonstrate Nordic people's unique closeness to forest nature. This was promoted to advance the idea of Germans as good forest people and Jews as rootless desert people, from which the forests must be protected.[27]

Third Reich landscape designers were honored for being specially gifted in interpreting nature and recreating it in their designs, and their work was considered of military importance. Governmental policies developed under this regime established landscape guidelines, such as the "Rules of Design for the Landscape."[28] These Rules required that landscapes contain only native plants and that they resemble a "close-to-nature" style. Alien plants were marked for extermination, and replaced with vegetation deemed native. Landscapes in public parks, along highways, and in rural areas became symbols of the Third Reich's good handling of nature; one that was better and morally superior to other people's. Meanwhile, front lawns of Jews removed to concentration camps were faithfully mowed by their neighbors, to complete the picture of living in harmony with nature.

It is important to remember that nature is not fascist or democratic. Rather, the authority and moral edification that comes with identifying with nature has been used to justify radically different political aims, whether forged from dictatorship or democracy.[29] During the same time period, nature protection and conservation in the United States was endowed with democratic sentiment. As a result of the dust bowl, Great Depression, and the resulting social and economic upheavals of the 1930s, the U.S. was also doubting the modern industrial project. Leopold considered nature conservation to be the seed of democratic thought—"proof" that democracy uses its land and natural processes "decently."[30]

SEEING LANDSCAPES AS LANDSCAPES

There is still the problem of what constitutes nature in a landscape. To experience the pull of the moon on a deserted beach during a winter evening's storm is to fulfill Budd's argument that nature should be seen as nature. The natural forces at the beach are so powerful that any human presence is insignificant. Yet, the thesis offered by Budd may also serve to further separate humans from nature. The likelihood of finding Budd's pure nature in our daily lives is rare because we are not only required to see nature as nature, but what we see must be nature untouched by humans.

We could redirect this "seeing as" to seeing landscapes as landscapes—both culture and nature. It is difficult to draw a line between nature and culture in landscapes, even ones brimming with vegetal life. Technological developments and cultural institutions, even fashion, consistently shape bio-logical elements, such as flowers. The British Colour Council, for example, defines color for machinery and clothing. Yet their color system is also used by the Royal Horticultural Society when they distinguish different cultivars of plants. In fact, horticulturalists working in the floral industry are the most eager to ascertain the color trends forecasted by color gurus, such as Pantone, because they need time to grow the right colored plants for the following season, and perhaps even create new hybrids. Likewise, appreciation for what is produced naturally and culturally is a two-way street. People

Figure 3.2 Camellia flower (photo credit: Susan Herrington)

may like the sound of flutes because it reminds them of song birds. Yet, they might equally delight in natural objects, such as the confectionery allure of a Camellia flower, because it looks human produced, nature appearing as artifice.

This oscillation between what we see as nature and what we see as culture is captured by artist Andy Goldsworthy. A photograph of his work with leaves at first glance looks to be a pile of green leaves that have a red circle painted on it. Upon closer inspection, you see Goldsworthy has painstakingly collected leaves of the same species, but some leaves have turned red and some have not. He has created the circle by filling the center of the image with red leaves. Finding red and green leaves of the same size, he tears them in half and fuses the green and red leaves together to form the edge of the red circle. Green leaves fill the rest of the image. The work is obviously human made and framed with the camera, but it does make me think about the radical color differentials found in leaves, and the bold designs that can be made with this natural material.

To see nature as nature—something that has not been purposefully designed for us—calls for empathy towards non-human concerns and a base from which to make decisions about the non-human world. Yet, there is no reason why empathy for humans should not be part of this seeing. This is why seeing landscapes as landscapes—not as nature, not as idealized myth, not as neutral system—can incorporate within the waves of environmental debates issues of social inequities, poverty, race, and gender. To see landscapes as landscapes, we must also understand how we interpret landscapes, and how they mean. This is the subject of the following chapters.

Four

RUINS THEN AND NOW
The Taste of Memory

Memory is the ability to recall past experiences—culturally or personally—in the present. It became critical to interpretations of landscapes during the eighteenth century when absolute standards on beauty and proportion forged in the Renaissance were supplanted by theories about taste. Since taste is variable and relies on interpretations made by the viewer, a viewer's memory became key in the cultivation of taste. This repositioning of the viewer from passive receptor to active participant shifted emphasis from *what* was being observed to *the observer*. Consider philosopher Archibald Alison's description of the sublime:

> No man acquainted with English history, could behold the field of Agincourt, without some emotion of this kind. The additional conceptions which this association produces, and which fill the mind of the spectator on the prospect of the memorable field, diffuse themselves in some measure over the scene, and give it a sublimity which does not actually belong to it.[1]

According to Alison, memories and associations create the field sublime. The famous field of Agincourt, where Henry V's troops defeated the French who outnumbered them three to one, is not sublime in and of itself. For some, the field will trigger memories that create feelings of adoration and reverence. Certain qualities of the field, such as being windy for instance, might heighten its sublimeness, but for Alison it is memory that makes it sublime. A person unfamiliar with English history or not moved by this particular story may draw different associations.

Since landscapes can contain tangible artifacts of the past, they have played a vital role in stimulating memories and associations. This idea was enthusiastically embraced in the design of eighteenth-century English landscapes. In the first section, these landscapes were critiqued for attempting to naturalize the power and wealth of their owners over the people who actually worked the land. Likewise, their formal qualities were also found to inhibit both what we think landscapes and nature should look like. Nonetheless, this ideological role and the formal aspects of these landscapes should not overshadow the ingenious way associations and memories were drawn from them.

Fascination with memory and landscapes during the eighteenth century was indebted to the publication of ancient literature, such as Virgil's poetry, increased exposure to Eastern aesthetics, and the Grand Tour taken by young British upperclass men. The Grand Tour through Italy provided the finishing touches to a university education. Through direct exposure to ancient Greek and Roman architecture, art, and landscape (such as the newly excavated city of Pompeii) young men were expected to return to England with a deeper understanding of ancient civilizations. An unintended effect of this edifying tour was the emulation of pastness—past empires, past virtues, past triumphs—in the landscapes created by these men upon their return to England.

Consider Henry Hoare II, who at the age of nineteen was called home early from a Grand Tour in Italy to run the affairs of his family's business, Hoare's Bank. Once settled in England, and after the death of two wives, Henry Hoare II dedicated himself to designing, with architect Henry Flitcroft, an extensive landscape, Stourhead, at his family estate in Wiltshire. After damming the estate's main river to create a large lake, he set up a circuitry of pathways connected by boating itineraries that brought visitors to a series of structures, such as the Temple of Flora, the Pantheon, Gothic ruins, a Grotto for bathing, and lastly the Temple of Apollo.

As visitors moved through this aqueous landscape, a combined story of two seemingly remote but similar pasts emerged —those of Aeneas, Virgil's classical hero and the mythic founder of Rome, and King Alfred the founder of England.

Figure 4.1 Henry Hoare II, Stourhead (photo credit: Susan Herrington)

According to philosopher Stephanie Ross, interpreting Stourhead involved a "two-foldedness" where certain features of the landscape were experienced simultaneously with the past to which it referred. "We see the central lake, know that it is a feature of the Wiltshire landscapes created in Henry Hoare's time, and we also know that in the world of iconography, it is the Lake Avernus," from Virgil's *Aeneid*.[2]

Similar to the field of Agincourt example, this interpretation described by Ross requires the viewer to be informed. Indeed during Hoare II's time a great emphasis was placed on cultivating a richly stored mind as a sign of taste. This enabled people to draw numerous and vivid associations from landscapes, whether encountered in the open countryside or within the exclusive confines of a private estate like Stourhead. Furthermore, writers and landscape gardeners devised complex theories explaining how this associative process worked.

Picturesque Association

Richard Payne Knight proposed one of the most influential theories for interpreting landscapes—picturesque association. Knight was an English classics scholar, Member of Parliament from 1780 to 1806, and the designer of his own picturesque estate Downton Castle. He thought that taste was informed by exposure to paintings and classical writings—particularly those by Virgil and Theocritus. Despite his adoration for ancient classics, it was Knight's emphasis on the observer's mind that defined his picturesque association.

In his publication *Analytical Inquiry into the Principles of Taste*, 1805, he laid the groundwork for his associative theory.[3] Knight acknowledged that the senses were a source of pleasure, what he called the "organic sense of vision;" however, his theory of picturesque association privileged the imagination and intellect in the formation of meaning, and ultimately taste. In Knight's view, if we acted purely on visual sensation— without intellect—we would be unable to enjoy the mottled condition of plaster on a wall in a Tuscan villa *over* the mottled condition of mold on the surface of last week's soup retrieved from the refrigerator. The mottled condition of the wall and the rotten soup would look the same. It is our intellect, perhaps remembering a bout with food poisoning, that tells us to enjoy the Tuscan wall over the soup.

Accordingly, Knight also thought that decipherment should be suspended in favor of savoring the perceptual experience and ruminating on associative rather than literal interpretations. He argued that the very act of "recollection enhances enjoyment and enjoyment brightens recollection."[4] This sentiment is articulated in Thomas Whateley's description of ruins in his *Observations on Modern Gardening* from 1770:

> At the sight of a ruin, reflections on the change, the decay, and the desolation before us, naturally occur; and they introduce a long succession of others, all tinctured with that melancholy which these have inspired: or if the monument revive the memory of former times, we do not stop at the simple fact which it records, but recollect many more coaeval circumstances, which we see not perhaps as they were, but as they are come down to us, venerable with age, and magnified by fame.[5]

For Whateley, the associations sparked by a ruin can lead to a range of "reflections on the change" or a "long succession" of feelings. He also demonstrates how interpretation surpasses simple recognition. Ruins do not merely "record," but release associations that "we do not see perhaps as they were, but as they come down to us."

Eighteenth-Century Ruins

Since the pleasure we receive from picturesque association takes place in the mind and not entirely in the object being perceived, this enabled landscapes previously considered unsightly to be enjoyed as picturesque. With picturesque association the ugly, the melancholy, and the grotesque were welcomed and enjoyable attributes of experiences with landscapes. Consequently, specific design features in these landscapes were intended to engage one's associative memory. Decaying Roman bridges, lichen-covered Greek temples, and dark grottoes triggered rumination on the lost glories of past civilizations. Rundown mills and hermit huts served as leitmotives of England's humble, agrarian society that lived from the land, prompting us to recall this way of life, and reflect upon the modesty that came with it.

Ruins in particular—either classical or vernacular—became the experiential space of the past, which could stimulate a range of sensations and associations ushered in by memory. In fact, if a property lacked existing ruins—perhaps the foundations of a Roman villa or an abandoned dovecote—they could be designed as sham ruins. A sketch by Kent depicting his design for a new crumbling mill demonstrates the calculation required to create such an edifice. Kent's drawings for the new ruin not only depict a roofless dilapidated structure made of chiseled stone, but to mimic the effects of time and gravity the structure is garnished with lichen and on the ground lies chunks of broken stones. While the structure was new, it was to be maintained in a state of decay—never completely gone, but always teetering on the brink of disintegration.

This use of ruins was a stark contrast to the role that structures and sculptures formerly played in landscapes. Previous landscapes from history referred to vernacular forms or classical motifs as timeless evocations of the past to be improved upon by the present. For example Renaissance villas boldly revived vernacular landscape elements, such as pergolas, water basins, and geometric garden plots. Articulating these elements as exemplary forms in an ideal state, they were also modified to accommodate new leisurely activities, such as masquerades and the viewing of plays and fireworks.

Or think of the fountains in the Baroque gardens of Versailles. The Fountain of Apollo, the centerpiece of the garden's east–west axis, renews this Olympian deity as the consummate embodiment of the Sun King himself. Apollo, the sun god and Louis XIV's mythological counterpart, emerges from the fountain on his gilded chariot in a glorious propulsion of water. Originally serviced by the Machine de Marly, one of the most daring hydrological feats of the seventeenth century, this ancient deity is revived in the splendor of its materials and design.

Post-industrial Ruins

But why are ruins and the picturesque theories of a cravat-wearing classical scholar relevant now? Interestingly, Knight's emphasis on our associations and memories, and the inclusion of the ugly and the melancholy in landscape appreciation are still valued. For example, some of the most provocative works of landscape architecture today frame deteriorating relics from our industrial past.

These are hulking industrial structures, which would have been deemed eyesores in earlier landscape creations. But now they are relished as potent content in the conversion of industrial sites to post-industrial parks, and associations of loss and decay are paramount to their interpretation and attraction.

Much like the eighteenth-century landscapes that lamented the loss of both classical glory and agrarian landscapes, parks created from industrial sites recall the loss of the West's industrial might from a twenty-first century service-oriented perspective.

One of the earliest and most adventuresome examples of a post-industrial park is Germany's Duisburg North Park designed by Peter Latz and Partners, landscape architects. Previously the site of the Thyssen factory, it was redesigned as a 200 hectare park in the 1990s. At Duisburg North, the abandoned railway scaffolding, blast furnaces, and foundry walls were all retained and function now like ruins in eighteenth century landscapes. Keeping the structures was not only more affordable than removing them, but it was also a goal of the designers to stimulate people's memory with their ruined presence in the park. Latz states "that instead of covering up memories, we sought to reveal what the rubble concealed."[6]

Duisburg North was critical in demonstrating that the remnant structures of the industrial age were now distant enough in time and space to trigger memories. Indeed to encounter Duisburg North Park is to encounter some forgotten land. Yet, it is pleasurable because the park's desolation is experienced through its art—its specific design—the way the industrial structures are maintained in a ruinous state, the intricate pathways, and the improbable activities that are boldly intervened into the site—and our interpretation of it. Detailed knowledge of the industrial revolution is not required, but an awareness of the transformative rise of mechanical power and large-scale industrial production of a unified Germany in the nineteenth century and its fall in the twentieth century give the park's ruinous state a sublimeness that does not necessarily belong to it.

Figure 4.2 Latz and Partners, Duisburg North (photo credit: Michael Latz)

Figure 4.3 Latz and Partners, Duisburg North (photo credit: Luca M. F. Fabris)

Visitors to Duisburg are struck by the fact that the whole park cannot be understood at a glance. The seemingly endless succession of immense decaying structures must be experienced by walking through and around them. Walking along the abandoned railway lines that organize movement throughout the park, people pass over huge bridges, haunted tunnels, and promontory points that frame views of this ruined city of iron and steel.

Succumbing to the forces of nature, the park's industrial relics act as ruins. Eroded metal replaces lichen-covered limestone, complex networks of conduit substitute for decorative treillage, and ruminations on the loss of virtues achieved in the classical era are replaced with musings upon the loss of the Ruhr Valley's industrial might to over-production, pollution, and foreign competition. Unlike many other European parks, there are no neatly kept grass lawns or beds of annuals heralding spring at Duisburg. Instead plants that absorb and covert toxins in the soil unabashedly coil and creep up the deteriorating structures, while patches of unruly birches alternate with slag piles along the canal.

Underscoring the importance of the imaginative liberty of visitors to the park, Latz notes that "these places of devastation offer much greater freedom of action, not only to landscape architects, but above all, the user."[7] Thus, activities at Duisburg North consciously invert the idea of dereliction, surprising the eye and the intellect. The gasometer becomes a scuba diving facility, the cooling trough a lily pond, and the blast furnace that lurks above the skyline accommodates a disco.

Former industrial sites are now not only reasonable areas to build parks, but desirable places for parks. This has influenced landscapes designed in North America as well, where industrial artifacts once deemed eyesores are now traces of the past to be savored as lost.[8] Consider the High Line, a 10 meter high abandoned rail-line that weaves through twenty-two blocks of Manhattan's west side. People's appreciation of this industrial structure's raw poetry and the overwhelming desire to relish it in its reincarnation as a park landscape is in debt to picturesque association.

Built in the 1930s to prevent collisions between trains, pedestrians, and automobiles, by the 1950s it was outmoded by the expanding trucking industry. Parts of the line were

Figure 4.4 High Line (photo credit: Joel Sternfeld © 2000, Courtesy of the Friends of the High Line)

torn down in the 1960s and in the 1980s the remaining line was abandoned. While many people thought it was unsightly and pushed for its removal, railroad enthusiasts consistently blocked the structure's complete erasure from the city.

For more than twenty years the remaining 2.5 kilometers of the High Line lay abandoned, open to the sky, and inaccessible by humans. This created an untouched wild corridor in the midst of Manhattan that by 2000 was crowned with a self-seeded ecosystem of vegetation and wildlife. Like a found ruin in an eighteenth-century landscape garden, this plant encrusted edifice is now valued for its patina as an industrial ruin ravaged by time and the vagaries of nature. Also like a ruin, the High Line triggers memories and associations about New York's industrial past, its former manufacturing glory now gone. This is a past that is far enough away in time for most New Yorkers to allow them to enjoy it as picturesque. Importantly, it also brings to light changes in the landscape

Figure 4.5 Field Operations and Diller Scofidio + Renfro, Proposal for The High Line (Courtesy of the City of New York)

that often go unnoticed, such as the dispersal of seeds by wind and birds.

Emotions

Since landscapes have a powerful ability to elicit a chain of memories and associations, they can also trigger strong emotions and feelings. Emotions and feelings featured heavily in eighteenth-century thinking from art to politics to science. In contrast, during the twentieth century emotions were held as the antithesis to rational thinking. Perhaps this is why some of the most emotive landscapes, such as cemeteries, were excluded from hallmark modernist landscapes like suburban developments.

Modern empirical studies of emotions and feelings were avoided in the sciences as well. Neuroscientist Antonio Damasio points out that "twentieth-century science left out the body, moved emotion back into the brain, but relegated it to the lower neural strata associated with ancestors who no one worshipped. In the end not only was emotion not rational, even studying it was probably not rational."[9] Yet, based on case studies of patients, Damasio proposes that emotions are directly tied to cognition, particularly with respect to aspects of interpretation, such as causal thinking. The re-emergence of emotions as consequential to thought is significant because certain types of landscapes, such as memorials, elicit emotional responses as central to their interpretation. Unlike post-industrial ruins, memorial landscapes arouse painful memories that are transformed by recollection, reflection, and even hope.

MEMORIALS
Signs of Life

Whereas ruins express the passage of time to trigger memories, many contemporary memorials don't express the past, nor do they express emotional states. Rather past memories are called forth to evoke an emotional state in the viewer. This reflects a change in the way the past is stimulated by landscapes, but also the art of memorial design itself.

While Jackson argued for historic monuments over experiential simulations of the past, memorial designs since the 1980s have consistently questioned the ability of heroic monuments to properly memorialize the catastrophic events of modernism—the World Wars, the Holocaust. In response, a new breed of memorials has emerged that emphasizes grim facts in a spatial experience that triggers emotional states in people. These new memorials also encourage participatory responses, such as the placement of personal items, as an equally emotive force in the experience. This transformation involves a skepticism of history itself. By emphasizing personal memories of the deceased, they question whose story history really explains and officiates.

Abandoning the heroic statuary of commemoration, Maya Lin's Vietnam Memorial in Washington D.C., was one of the first of these memorial landscapes. Lin's "silent" black granite wall, which stirred a flood of emotional responses, heightened the way the physical exterior world tugs at the psychological interior. Unlike other memorials in Washington D.C., Lin's design draws you below grade. You physically become part of the memorial, traveling downward past the rote chronology of deaths, witnessing your reflections captured in the gaps between their names. By inverting military rank for chronological time, the names accumulate in number as the wall descends. Although each inscribed name is only 1.35 centimeters in size, there are so many that they stack to a height of 3 meters at the turning point of the wall.

Many people visiting the memorial do not personally know anyone who died in Vietnam. But public memory of the quantity of death is grounded by memories of the veterans themselves evidenced by the placement of items at the wall each day. There are flags and commemorative floral displays, but it is the personal items of the veterans that affect you the most. These are the unanswered cards and letters, birth announcements of children they would never meet, and the faded photographs of unfinished men who smile at you unaware of their horrific fate.

The Vietnam Memorial also provoked controversy. Two years after its construction, the Soldiers' Memorial was installed featuring figurative sculptures of soldiers that expressed for us their heroism and their plight. Nonetheless, the wall changed the way we memorialize and spurred numerous design competitions where designers and artists continue to vie in their ability to artfully stimulate emotions in direct proportion to the tragedy being framed.

Sites of Memory

Since landscapes can be the literal ground of tragic events, context has increasingly become paramount to physically marking memory in place for emotive effect. For example, the memorial at the site of the former World Trade Center towers in New York City must be at the location where approximately 2752 people perished. Despite the bottom-line ethos of Manhattan real-estate, the main memorial to 9/11 needs to be on the land between Church, West, Vesey, and Liberty Streets. That particular spot on the earth cannot be substituted for another more convenient or less expensive location in the city.

It appears that the creation of memorial landscapes has become an enduring part of the memorializing process. Six years after the attacks, 74 percent of registered voters wanted to see progress made on the memorial at the site of the former twin towers.[10] As of this writing the selected memorial design by Michael Arad and Peter Walker has not been completed. However, its success as a landscape of significance will reside in its ability not to simply prompt my interpretation of the memorial as an expression of sadness regarding this horrific event. Rather the memorial's success lies in its ability to make me *be* sad, as a way of not forgetting the memory of this event.

The unification of Germany and the controversy surrounding Germany's history of itself has also fueled the creation of numerous memorial landscapes. A poignant example that mixes official record with social memory is the Bavarian Quarter (Bayerische Viertel) in Berlin. Designed by artists Renata Stih and Frieder Schnock, this memorial is embedded into the every-day signs of a residential neighborhood. Signaling that the official history is but a cautionary guide to the future, it fuses the spatial qualities of this urban landscape with the obligations to remember the past.

Before World War II, this neighborhood was home to many Jews, some famous like Albert Einstein and Hannah Arendt. Yet, the former presence of Jews in this neighborhood had been erased and never acknowledged in the history of the city. Revealing how deadly moves are rendered neutral through the language of law, the artists placed throughout the quarter eighty sign posts each listing an anti-Jewish law and the date it was enacted between 1933 and the 1940s. For example, one sign states the 1938 law that "Aryan and non-Aryan children are not allowed to play together." Another sign says "Jews may inherit only when the national socialist morals are upheld" and another reads "Anti-Semitic signs in Berlin will be temporarily removed for the 1936 Olympic Games."[11]

The Bavarian Quarter memorial does not participate in the tradition of expressive works that are shaped to mimic the emotions they seek to evoke. Like the Vietnam Memorial, factual information heightens an emotional response. The memorial "signs" are created in the most perfunctory fashion with black Times Roman text on a white anonymous background. On the reverse side of each sign, is an accompanying logo that recalls the graphics associated with the most basic public amenities denoting when it is safe to walk, who should use the toilet facilities, and compliant wheelchair accessibility.

Its emotional power stems from the way it grasps how seemingly ordinary life—as one walks through this quiet neighborhood—is shaped by public laws that often lie outside personal control, but depend on personal awareness and debate to keep it just. Moreover, it highlights in the time and space between the signs the incremental ways in which fascism germinates from the inside of a society—through its laws that govern daily life from by-laws to signage.

Spontaneous Memorials

Importantly, non-designers create landscapes that trigger memories and intense emotion. This is evident in the rise of spontaneous memorials commemorating car accidents, bombings, and school shootings—dedicated to the famous as well as the unknown. There is no professional planning involved in these memorials; rather, their creation as a matter of collective impulse accentuates their emotive power.

Sometimes sheer manyness gives us the emotional gravity evoked by spontaneous memorials. Consider the eruption of mass emotion after Princess Diana's death in a car crash. The spontaneous memorial that emerged seemed to relocate every available flower in England to the gates of Kensington Palace. These were bouquets placed by the over two million people who pilgrimaged there to mourn her death. By the end of the week, the flowers filled the entire entry court to the palace creating a sensory field of rustling cellophane and faded color.

Spontaneous memorials to the unfamous involve the placement of everyday objects of the deceased much like the Vietnam Wall. Consider the spontaneous memorial that materialized at the site of the Oklahoma City Bombing where 168 people died. The chain-link fence surrounding the empty lot where the bombed Alfred P. Murrah federal building once stood became the sacred site where people brought items to display.

Visiting the Oklahoma site, you are immediately struck by the number and variety of articles, which despite the efforts of volunteers who regularly prune it, outsize the humbleness of the fence itself. These items included blurry photographs of people at office parties, personal notes of words never said, faded T-shirts, plastic flowers, children's drawings, old stuffed animals, gruffy baseball caps, school photos, and worn shoes. In any other context these items would hardly be fodder for a yard sale. However, the banality of these objects—the way we took them for granted when they were Vince's cap or Dustin's obligatory school photo—endow their transformation as permanent fragments of life's impermanence.

Figure 4.6 Oklahoma City Bombing Memorial Fence (photo credit: Susan Herrington)

Spontaneous memorials also point to a need in contemporary landscapes to acknowledge death, not as a planned "land use," but as a place formed by collective ritual. Art Historian Harriet F. Senie writes that spontaneous memorials created at places such as the Oklahoma City fence and Columbine High School reveal how the emotive markings of life and death have been edited out of contemporary landscapes. These memorials fill the gap of the hallowed ground of cemeteries and the ritual practices they espoused. "Although the bodies are buried elsewhere, almost every detail of the spontaneous memorial revives the role cemeteries historically played in public life. The dead were once buried in the center of town, where they became a daily reminder of the fate awaiting us all."[12] Currently, actual cemeteries have been zoned out to the distant peripheries of most cities, and they are rarely a component to small town or residential developments. Most people typically die in the sanitized confines of a hospital. Memorials—

spontaneous or designed—revive the very human need to acknowledge our dead.

Memorial landscapes and contemporary ruins share a similar trait in their expression. Some of the most powerful memorials, such as the Vietnam War Memorial Wall, or the spontaneous memorials, give us only fragments of information regarding the people they commemorate. Likewise, the functions of the derelict structures at Duisburg are largely unknown to us, so they make us wonder—what was that huge blast furnace really used for? These landscapes of memory leave ample room for us to fill in a train of thoughts and emotions. In other words, their significance is understood as it is ushered in by the imagination.

Five

IMAGINATION
The Work of Imagination

Imagination plays an important role in activating memories because it enables us to form mental images about events, things, or people that are not present. Yet, the increasing barrage of ready-made images that saturate daily life may have eroded our ability to imagine. Indeed, the authors of *New Keywords* caution that external images have helped eradicate imagination from our cerebral cortex, noting that the

> sweeping devaluation and incapacitation of a human ability
> to generate one's own images (or imagination) is inseparable
> from the ascendancy of already manufactured external
> images, which increasingly become the impersonal raw
> material of psychic life and determine the formal conditions
> of all so-called mental images.[1]

Studies concerning contemporary childhood, the critical time span when our ability to imagine is formed, confirm this condition. Children imagine through play, but the outdoor play spaces created for children's play increasingly lack the elements necessary to encourage imagination, such as mystery or materials that can be shaped and formed, such as mud.

A study of children's outdoor play spaces in Canada found

that play areas with ample malleable materials provided for more imaginative play than newer play spaces featuring stationary pre-fabricated play structures. Many of these play structure environments are imagined by playground manufacturers to symbolize play for adult consumers, but they don't necessarily encourage children to imagine. They don't capture the way children can turn a discarded box into a spaceship or a hedge into a house. When children create something from what it is not, a house from a thicket of hedges for example, they invent in their minds the walls, doors, and windows of their houses using their imagination.

Perhaps we have a romantic notion of childhood, when children built sand castles and forts, creating their own worlds as an extension of the mind. So what if we can no longer imagine? According to developmental psychologist Paul Harris, imagination is not only important in the creation of mental images, but the ability to put these images to use is a basic skill that we employ throughout our lives. Imagination forged during childhood is linked to the development of causal judgments, moral reasoning, and language comprehension in adulthood.[2] In this sense, imagination is instrumental to how we understand the world and conduct ourselves in it.

Instrumental Imagination

Unlike the picturesque appeal to the mnemonic and emotive interpretations of landscapes, instrumental imagination is strategic because it can aid in understanding and making decisions about landscapes. However, like picturesque association, it allows landscapes once considered undesirable to be valuable. For example, wetlands in North America were traditionally thought to be wastelands—unarable spaces harboring diseases and unpleasant looking creatures. European settlers avoided them, but they were systematically drained throughout the nineteenth and early twentieth centuries to create arable land. Now that we know wetlands play a vital role in cleaning water, mitigating flood conditions, and providing habitat to numerous plant and animal species they are appreciated both visually and functionally. Wetlands are now highly sought-after features in gardens and parks. This is also true of water treatment facilities like Brightwater. Water treatment plants have a high degree of functionality, but undesirable associations for people—they are what Thayer deemed real landscapes. Yet, now they can be designed as parks for people to enjoy and interpret.

The instrumental imagination can also help us make sense of complex landscapes such as cities. This is the beauty of Kevin Lynch's classic study, *Image of the City* (1960).[3] Lynch wanted to know which elements of the urban landscape allowed people to understand and navigate through it. Interviewing people in Los Angeles, Boston, and Jersey City, he found that people used specific features to create mental representations or mental maps of what the city contained and the way it was organized. These features included paths, edges, districts, nodes, and landmarks. The clarity and prominence of these features in urban landscapes, Lynch concluded, increased people's ability to imagine the city.[4]

Lastly, the instrumental imagination can also allow us to make mental models of aspects of a landscape we can't experience first hand. Harris stresses that imagination enables us to construct alternative scenarios and make linkages between things we will never encounter. Narratives involve a type of instrumental imagination that can help us visualize events that we are unable to experience directly. For example, we cannot experience Europe's industrial revolution face to face, so it comes to us in the form of stories expressed in words or sometimes in landscapes, such as Duisburg North. Narratives are imagined, even non-fictional narratives, and they can be created by the designer/author, reader or both.

NARRATIVE
Common Landscapes

The efficacy of landscapes to frame time in space make them powerful sites for narration. Narratives are important because they can help us see elements in landscapes as a series of temporal sequences. They can explain change over time in ways that other models cannot—even about the most mundane spaces of our lives. Walk down any street in your neighborhood and you can create a story. This is what Jackson did so well with common or what he called vernacular landscapes. Through his interpretations of the shapeless banality of suburban housing, strip-malls, highways, and motor-courts he gave meaning to the everyday landscapes that prior to his writing were not worthy of study.

Consider his narrative recounting the domestic garage. He describes how different types of garages, "now almost essential to the family dwelling," tell a story about the concept of home.[5] For example, the Romantic Garage of a 1910 house was the sanitized refuge of the family's expensive toy—the car. It was isolated from the house in the rear of the property and distinct from any structures that might contain animals. While designed for efficiency, this dignified structure and the car it sheltered were not part of the idea of home. However, it was sometimes designed to emulate the Colonial, Tudor, or Craftsman styles of the main house, attesting to the homeowner's intelligence and taste.

The Practical Garage arose as a "small portable and pre-fabricated structure" easy to access and located at the rear of the property. Combined with a fence, the garage helped to hide the back yard which contained ashes from the furnace, the dog house, and the daily clutter of the clothes line. For Jackson, the Practical Garage of the 1930s was a transition point between the home as the locus of high-minded and educational endeavors and the 1970s concept of the home as a place for recreation and fun.[6]

By the 1950s the Family Garage is "thoroughly integrated into the street facade of the house—to the point where its wide doors serve to balance the picture window."[7] The notion of home as the site for entertainment became so pervasive by the 1970s that most of these garages were converted into TV rooms, dens, and recreation rooms; leaving cars out in the driveways.

While Jackson's story ends in the 1970s, we can carry the narrative forward. With the development of new urbanist housing, there is a revival of the freestanding garage at the rear of the yard, accessed by the alley. This garage is a massive structure often spanning the entire width of the lot. It completely blocks, both physically and visually the backyard, the place which confines the children. While it is designed to match the historically inspired style of the house, its long opaque electric door is absent of windows or any signs of what lies behind it. Graced with security cameras and alarm systems, this could be called the Defense Garage, representing the idea of home as secure fortress, which protects traditional values.

Narratives in History

The history of landscapes is steeped in narrative from the elaborate metonymy of Renaissance landscapes to the unbridled intricacy of Chinese scholar gardens to the sequential unfolding of space and time in Japanese stroll gardens. One of the most famous garden narratives is the stroll garden at Katsura Rikyu Imperial Villa in Kyoto. The garden was made by Prince Toshihito between 1620 and 1658 on an old family estate along the Katsura River. A great admirer of the eleventh-century prose fiction, The Tale of Genji[8] by Lady Murasaki Shikibu, the Prince sought to convey parts of this story through scenes in his garden.

There are striking similarities between Toshihito's own life and the fictional life of Genji. Like Genji, Toshihito's early life was marked by humiliation and disappointment, which left him "haunted by the impermanence of worldly things."[9] Also like Genji, who resolved to build a rural retreat near the village of Katsura for his mistress of dignified but humble birth, the Prince, after marrying for love over financial prosperity, dedicated the rest of his life to creating Katsura.

The intricate pathways, hills, waterways, bridges, gateways, and other structures Toshihito created at Katsura frame vignettes that resonate with the scenes described in The Tale of Genji. Entering the villa estate today, it is impossible to understand the whole garden at once. Like a story, it unfolds as people stroll. Just as lines on a page guide the movement of the eye, a path system of over 1700 stepping stones guide people through the main spatial sequences and views of the garden.

Moving in a clockwise direction around the large pond laden with planted islands and craggy peninsulas, visitors can imagine specific places in the text. For example, the Shoka-Tei tea house with its lanterns, whose reflections glow in the pond below, refers to the chapter where a young girl's beauty is revealed by the glow of worms contained in Genji's paper

Figure 5.1 Katsura (photo credit: Dominic McIver Lopes)

sack. In another chapter, Genji encounters at the "waiting pine tree" an unrequited lover who he has all but forgotten, and this is recalled by the lone pine that waits at the edge of the pond at Katsura.

The atmosphere portrayed in the book and Katsura are also similar. The entire garden evokes the Japanese aesthetic of kirei sabi—elegant rustic simplicity. The avoidance of ostentatious materials and ornate structures in favor of weathered wood, thatched rooftops, moss, and untouched stones reflects Toshihito's and Genji's suspicion of wealth. The seventy-four lanterns placed throughout the garden and the borrowed view of the moon from the main pavilion reinforce the romantic nighttime use of gardens in the story as well. Likewise, the abundant plants, such as maples, whose colors announce autumn, also serve as references. They allude to the many deaths that pervade the story—his mother, his mistresses, and before the narrative ends, his own.

While most visitors today are unaware of the garden's literary connections, Toshihito's garden gives us a refined beauty and exquisiteness that you cannot resist, an underlying theme in Genji's tale. This landscape narrative also provides a sequence of different views and spaces that pace imagination. For example, Toshihito's careful choreography of "the stroll" as an underlying narrative structure yields a continually unfolding garden that keeps visitors in constant anticipation of what is to come next. Katsura not only became the model for later stroll gardens, but demonstrated that the experience of a garden, like a story, can be orchestrated in time by movement.

Narratives Now

By the twentieth century many landscape architects abandoned narrative; however, during the past thirty years it has been recovered as a central trope for the instrumental imagination. This revival is largely in debt to earthworks, minimalist works, and public art. Artists creating these works often use the same material as landscape architects—earth, water, sun, shadow, plants, rocks, concrete, manufactured objects, and context. However, they employ these materials and their context to tell a story. In turn, their emphasis on the communicative powers of materials prompted landscape architects to employ narratives in their designs for landscapes.[10] Landscape narratives can expand our imagination in three important ways.

Revealing What is Hidden

Since landscape narratives can help us imagine events that we don't normally encounter, they can also help us imagine things that are literally hidden from our first-hand experiences with landscapes. The Bamboo Garden, designed by landscape architect Alexander Chemetoff, makes this poignantly clear. In this sunken garden at Parc de la Villette in Paris, Chemetoff exposes and incorporates water mains and electrical lines that run through the park. This is the type of infrastructure that sustains both the park and the surrounding neighborhoods, and links them to the meta-infrastructure of Paris. While these types of conduits are essential to the park's functioning they are typically buried underneath the soil, absent from our experience and knowledge of Parc de la Villette.

Descending into this garden you are not only taken by its coolness and the fecund growth of the lush bamboo, but the immensity of the conduits that traverse over head. These are huge pipes that crisscross over this grotto-like space in alignments whose bearings lie elsewhere—to distant buildings or a far away treatment plant. At the base of the garden a sound chamber designed by Bernhard Leitner takes environmental sounds of the garden—bird songs, wind, perhaps the sound of fluids moving through pipes—and mixes them into a haunting melody that echoes throughout the garden.

Witnessing all this massive infrastructure that lies below

On Landscapes

Figure 5.2 Alexandre Chemetoff, Parc de la Villette (photo credit: Kate B. Notman)

the surface of the park, the Bamboo Garden entices you to imagine all the pipes that must run under the seemingly thin surface of a city. This one garden tells a story about how thick our urban landscapes really are—often several stories deep in systems that remain invisible to us—but as Chemetoff and Leitner demonstrate are as captivating as what lies above. This is important to imagine because it counters the camouflage role that landscapes often play in hiding infrastructure.

Narratives can also be critical. They can provide Dewey's resistance to what is expected. This is a central theme in the work of artist Ian Hamilton Finlay, whose motto is "certain gardens are described as retreats when they are really attacks."[11] In 1966 he began his own garden, now called Little Sparta, in Dunsyre, Scotland. Little Sparta's resistance lies in the fact that it does not appear as what it is. At first glance it is simply a 2 hectare pastoral landscape of seemingly innocuous garden tableaus with names like the Allotment Garden, the English Park Garden, and the Wild Garden. Yet, Little Sparta is also covered with over two hundred inscribed bridges, temple-like structures, decapitated columns, and other sculptures that play on the irony of words, objects, and spaces. The garden spaces together with these sculptures reveal a complex and often contradictory narrative.

The plot of this garden's story regards out instinct for self-preservation that has manifested itself in peculiar ways in Western culture—the best being to improve upon the nature of things and the worst that of warfare. For example, one of Finlay's earliest interventions was the placement of a wooden sign on a tree reading, MARE NOSTRUM. This is a phrase used by the Romans—at their height of dominance—to refer to the Mediterranean as "our sea." While this intervention highlights the dual life of hegemony—one that is both a powerful form of coercion, but seemingly natural and a matter of common sense—it also prompts you to listen to the tree itself. The sound of the rustling leaves that resembles the sound of a distant sea suggests that appearances and language are not what they always seem. That a tree can share similarities with a sea, recalls the ancient Greek idea that change happens only at the level of appearances. The real material of

Figure 5.3 Ian Hamilton Finlay, Little Sparta (photo credit: Mike Forsyth, Calligrafix)

things are the same, only rearranging themselves into new compositions that paint the world of appearances.

Another striking intervention is a formal garden entryway entitled Hypothetical Gateway to an Academy of Mars, created with David Ewick. The two pillars that frame this seemingly harmless gate appear to be topped with finials in the shape of large pineapples. Actual pineapples were used as symbols in Colonial times to signal "welcome" and later rendered in Coade stone as decorations in Victorian gardens. Upon closer inspection, visitors realize that what they thought were pineapples, really depict large grenades.

Substituting something we expect with something we don't expect—warnings for welcomes, destruction for decor—Little Sparta functions much like poetry. It supports Hunt's claim that gardens are to landscapes as poetry is to writing—the way that a poem can make us reconsider the entire English language—its insistence on a particular model, a set of associations, and the traditional role of reader and author. Finlay invites us to critique gardens—their persistence as a polite and comely art, their association with harmony and goodness, and most importantly their traditional role as retreats.

Narratives in the Design Process

Lastly, a major difference between twenty-first-century landscape narratives and ones from history is the use of storytelling as part of the design process; an act that can transfigure social relations and space. Landscape architects Matthew Potteiger and Jamie Purinton propose that storytelling can provide a framework for integrating people in the design process of landscapes.[12] By working with people whose stories are often excluded from the conventional histories of landscapes, such as the elderly, Potteiger and Purinton use storytelling to inform their design work. This approach not only reflects concerns with the author, but it also offers a counter to the questionnaire approach of integrating public views—which can result in least objectionable, rather than most wanted landscapes.

An example of narrative put into practice can be found in the work of landscape architect Walter Hood. Hood not only excels at getting people to tell stories about the landscapes he designs for them—parks, streets, schoolyards, and play-rounds—but he is also a good listener and observer of stories. His redesign for Lafayette Square in Oakland California evolved from a process of months of conversations with neighborhood residents. The park had physically deteriorated since its original inception during the nineteenth century, but he discovered that despite its deleterious condition people could still imagine it as a better place, and one reflecting more types of people than its current users.

The square had predominantly become home to men who were unemployed as well as homeless people—neighbors referred to them as the regulars. Hood worked closely with neighbors who did not use the park, and he also befriended the regulars as well. For Hood

> Our biggest set of ideas came out of trying to understand how the park evolved over time: why it fell into disrepair and the political, social, and economic issues. . . . then, instead of erasing everything, to begin to layer new ideas on the old. The park became a collage of ideas dealing with history, but in a very formal way.[13]

This refusal to erase what Lafayette was unofficially (officially it was one of the oldest Victorian parks in the Bay Area), enabled the design to accommodate uses relevant to the current culture. In fact, unlike many North American urban parks, the redesign of Lafayette Square included 24-hour services for homeless people. Hood also included spaces for drying clothes, children's play, barbecues, playing chess, tai chi, and hanging out.

Narratives are excellent for imagining change over time, but there is also a need to understand the way the animate physical elements of a landscape function with each other. According to Carlson, our ability to interpret a landscape's science—its geology, plant life, and hydrological system—is paramount. His gravitation towards the sciences suggests a need for an in-depth knowledge derived through experimentation, observation, and study. In contrast to Knight who thought people should be knowledgeable in the arts, Carlson contends that scientific knowledge, not the contemplation of landscapes as static scenes, will yield the better interpretation of it.[14]

Just as a classical music aficionado will offer a more rigorous interpretation of a piece of classical music than a person unacquainted with this music, a limnologist will be able to succinctly imagine conditions about a lake—such as why algae is forming in it—better than an average recreational boater. While both limnologist and boater can enjoy the lake, it is the limnologist's in-depth interpretation that Carlson argues is necessary for us to seriously imagine landscapes.[15]

While Carlson asks us to understand landscapes deeply, there are challenges to this proposal. For example, what about children who have not acquired an in-depth understanding of science? Will their lack of knowledge inhibit their ability to understand a landscape? Interestingly, this is where landscapes have a long tradition of being valued for their heightened capacity to teach.

The nineteenth-century inventor of the kindergarten, Friedrich Froebel, thought that changes taking place in landscapes and gardens offered tangible moments for children's learning. Combining songs, games, and daily observations of the kindergarten's gardens (which were integral to his original educational system) he was able to convey complex connections about the external environment—ideas we now name ecological systems. For example, he was less concerned that children learn the scientific nomenclature of bird species, rather he wanted children to think of birds in

> reference to the time of their appearance; yielding ideas of spring, summer, and fall flowers etc . . . The swallow is recognized as a summer bird, the lark as a spring bird etc.[16]

Indeed, bird migration is a complex system to map, but by linking repeated experiences over time, he enabled children to imagine the relationship between birds and the seasons.

Presaging the idea of seeing landscapes as landscapes, Froebel's interpretive walks were not lessons in plant and wildlife identification either. Rather, he used what children encountered on their walk to engender curiosity and discovery about the relationship among elements in a landscape. Pausing on a hilltop overlooking a small town, he would ask children what they saw. Once they perceived the organizational pattern of the town, this would lead to questions about why it was arranged that way. Why was the largest building in the center, for example.[17] Froebel's kindergarten pedagogy is an interesting model because his gardens and excursion activities were designed for an uninitiated audience, children.

Structural Models

Unfortunately, we can't always imagine landscape functions through direct experience. Structural models are representations of relationships among a set of variables that enable us to imagine how these variables are causally related to one another. Such models can help us imagine relationships among features in the physical world that we cannot understand face to face, such as ground water movement and bedrock. The ability to imagine how landscape features relate to each other became increasingly critical as awareness of human impacts on ecological systems heightened in the twentieth century.

Many ecological relationships are not always evidenced by first-hand experiences, particularly in the case of a large, complex landscape, such as a region. By the late 1960s, structural models of ecological relationships—both human made and naturally occurring—became valuable as a way to imagine and make decisions about complex landscapes. Structural models are well suited to this because they reveal working relationships among landscape features, and this in turn enables us to identify existing and potential causes and effects among these features.

In the 1960s and 1970s landscape architect Ian McHarg pioneered one of the most influential structural models used to design landscapes, the map overlay system. His system enabled designers to imagine the intersection of a diverse range of information over a site by spatially collapsing it onto one surface—the map. Acting as a kind of cognitive prostheses, it allowed for the correlation of patterns of opportunities and constraints among vastly different features, for example historic buildings and aquatic habitats. It helped designers determine where major landscape elements like houses and roadways should be located, and which features of a site should be preserved. McHarg's map system also enabled decisions to be made with an alacrity unmatched by simply thinking about it.

Structural models that explain how parts of a landscape relate to each other can help dissipate the ideological distortion discussed in Chapter 4. These models also supposedly

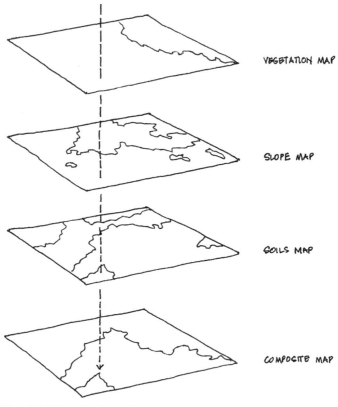

VEGETATION MAP

SLOPE MAP

SOILS MAP

COMPOSITE MAP

Figure 5.4 McHarg Map Overlay System

relieved designers of the authorship question because they enabled them to present their work as an objective product of data analysis. However, mapping is not an exclusively object-ive process as it requires decisions by the human author to determine what should be included in the map. In fact, the seemingly autonomous, sieve-like design method envisioned by McHarg can obscure the fact that a great deal of deci-sion making is still in human hands. Nonetheless, McHarg established the use of structural models as a method of imagining landscapes.

The subsequent importation of McHarg's method into computer systems has allowed for the inclusion of human actions as another overlay in a series of landscape forecasts. This not only reveals the designer's role in the design process, but challenges the representational problem of landscapes as static pictures of nature discussed in Chapter 3. Since the computer can animate change over time, landscapes can be imagined as a series of dynamic processes with elements that continually effect each other, changing over time.

Fresh Kills

With the overlay system operating in the digital world, we can make long-term projections about a landscape with image-editing, three-dimensional modeling, and animation programs. For example, a computer animated process is part of the redesign of one of the world's biggest landfills, Fresh Kills, located on the western banks of Staten Island. At 890 hectares, Fresh Kills is a dramatic landscape of winding waterways, flat alluvial wetlands, and hulking mountains engorged with household waste that climb to heights of 69 meters.

In 2003, after more than fifty years of filling, the land was dedicated as future park land. According to the project's lead landscape architect, James Corner, the solution to Fresh Kills park is a "strategy, not a design in any rigid sense."[18] The design forecasts the site as a thirty year metamorphosis of ecological processes. Animated diagrams of the biophysical and cultural movements over time help people imagine what the landscape is really like, and what it could be like. Some examples of these metamorphoses include mountain biking and BMX competition courses, plant succession, mating frogs, and parking cars that occupy the site and influence each other, continually adapting over time.

Yet, the question remains—will people actually using Fresh Kills interpret its dynamic processes—or do they even possess the knowledge or desire to understand how the park functions? It's unclear whether the complex orchestration of bio-physical and cultural processes at Fresh Kills will really reach the BMX riders and other park users. This is a salient point because an important dimension of landscapes is the way people interpret and imagine them to be.

Landscapes that trigger the instrumental imagination rely on the assumption that they will shape the way people think about the world and interact with it, forming what they believe. The philosopher William James contended that belief is not based on simply evidence and a desire to believe. Indeed if it was, no one would smoke or eat junk food because there has been ample information—data as well as anecdotes—that attest to the fact that theses activities are not healthy. For James, belief is informed by experiences. We can't simply want to believe in something, we must feel it is true.[19] This places our experiences with landscapes at the heart of why they matter.

Six

EVOLUTIONARY THEORIES
Evolutionary Blueprints

Evolutionary theories are frequently used to describe experiences with landscapes. Geographer Jay Appleton's *The Experience of Landscape*,[1] which introduces his theory of "prospect refuge" has proved the most persevering. Prospect refuge theory links contemporary navigation of space with our hunter–gatherer past. Coalescing millions of years of terrestrial life, Appleton's theory suggests that today's humans move through landscapes in a quest for survival and shelter no differently than early bipedal hominids. For instance, we seek prospects in a landscape so that we can see potential hazards, and we seek refuge to hide from them. In combination a prospect refuge landscape is a place where we can both see without being seen—a key location for survival. Appealing to a broad spectrum of disciplines, Appleton's theory has been applied in landscape architecture to create safer urban spaces, and even in architecture for the hospitality industry.

Seizing the empirically based approach of Appleton, and perhaps that of Komar and Melamid, environmental psychologists Rachel and Steven Kaplan have advanced the idea of environmental preference as the driver of our experiences with landscapes.[2] Environmental preference theory holds that we innately prefer certain landscapes because they contribute to our survival. Like Appleton, the Kaplans connect patterns across time, linking evolutionary blueprints of behavior with the way we engage the complex milieu of contemporary landscapes. The Kaplans' basic premise is that landscapes are communicators of information, and our behaviors in landscapes are comprised of information processing tasks, such as understanding and exploring. In short, they theorize that we prefer a landscape scene that satisfies our desire and this desire stems from our ability to process its information.

This theory has been confirmed by exposing people to images of landscapes, which were then weighted for preference, indicating that high-information processing pictures were preferred over pictures of other landscapes. Although the pictures used seldom feature other humans, frequent inhabitants of many landscapes, their methods have been hugely influential in identifying preferences about what landscapes, such as public parks, should look like.

The notion of innate landscape preferences is also advanced by ornithologist Gordon Orians and psychologist Judith Heerwagen.[3] They asked subjects to rate landscape paintings to determine if humans were wired to prefer landscapes that resemble the African Savannah, the presumed cradle of human origins. They found that people consistently liked the African Savannah best. Orians even suggests that we like flowers because they have long been associated with the food of our early ancestors. He writes, "in species-rich environments, paying attention to flowering plants may particularly enhance resource acquisition abilities in the future."[4]

It's curious how our innate food-recognition abilities account for the allure of numerous poisonous flowers like the lovely Calla Lily, which grows in Africa. Nonetheless, evolutionary theories of landscape experience offer counter-claims to the Kantian notion of disinterestedness, whereby any aesthetic interest that we have in a landscape cannot be based on its practical use. They link a highly utilitarian view of landscapes as a source of survival with the pleasure we receive from them. Accordingly, when I experience a landscape that offers prospect and refuge I find it pleasing.

However, these theories only tell us part of the story about how we experience landscapes. Like Danto's conclusion regarding the *Most Wanted Series*—that calendar art plays a bigger role in preference than an *a priori* biologically determined preference—evolutionary theories omit the powerful role of culture in forming preferences for landscapes like the African Savannah.[5] Indeed there are numerous cultural practices, poetry for example, in addition to calendar art that have intervened since our hunter–gatherer past to make admiring certain landscapes appealing.

Philosopher Denis Dutton adds that evolutionary theories cannot distinguish what is great art. "A painting of a desolate, arid, and uninviting landscape may be a much greater work of art than a calendar photograph of a green valley of the sort our Pleistocene ancestors might have most wanted to explore and inhabit."[6] Likewise, these theories don't tell us how landscapes are brilliantly portrayed in a painting, such as J.M.W. Turner's *Rain, Steam and Speed* (1844) or designed physically, such as Alain Provost's Barrier Park. Consider Shakespeare's *Romeo and Juliet*. What distinguishes it as a great play is not the content that might be deemed useful to our ancestors, such as warning us about the disastrous effects of flirting with a member of a rival clan in sixteenth-century Italy. What is significant are the effects of Shakespeare's art on our experience of the play—the way he crafts the English language in rhymed verse and the way he portrays fate, power, and love triumphing *over* human survival.

Making Sense

Experiences based on two-dimensional representations do not tell us much about first-hand experiences with three-dimensional landscapes and the specific attributes of these experiences. Many preference studies are based on people's experiences with two-dimensional pictures rather than experiences with actual landscapes, so they omit powerful dimensions of landscape experience, such as thermal comfort, smell, sound, taste, and tactile sensation.

Moreover, many landscapes are intentionally designed to communicate via a range of senses, which are absent when presented only two-dimensionally. Think of the rich variety of scents found in the Rosaceae family of an Edwardian rose garden. While beautiful to look at, a two-dimensional picture of such a rose garden could not capture the experience of smelling this garden. Returning to the African Savannah, given its proximity to the equator and lack of shade, perhaps a face-to-face experience with a Savannah would yield a different ranking from its picture.

Also, sense experiences are inextricably linked to what and how we think. The philosopher David Hume argued that thoughts were made of perceptions—the things we feel, sense, see, hear, taste, and smell. For Hume "ideas are not purer forms of sensations, but on the contrary, merely the fainter replica of these impressions."[7] It is our visceral interactions with the world that form our ideas about it. Hume's theories are relevant because, like other art forms, landscapes don't always carry literal messages, but can trigger sensations. This can be both their appeal and their power.

Sensorial qualities of landscapes that pull at our unconscious can lead to a vast range of feelings linked to sensations, such as hearing bubbling water as relaxing or biking down a steep hill as exhilarating. The smell of pine trees or water turning into steam on a hot pavement can recall specific points in time or an association or feeling. In a scent–recall study researchers found that people born in the 1930s and 1940s tended to recall memories stimulated by smells like burning leaves and cut grass, whereas people born in the 1960s and 1970s selected commercial and primarily interior smells like window cleaner as memory triggering.[8] Thus, smell preferences have changed in just a few decades.

There have also been studies that involve first-hand experiences with landscapes. Medical doctor and landscape architect Joanne Westphal conducted a two-year study at an elder home to document how experiences in a garden affected the health of the home's eighteen late-stage Alzheimer's patients. Data collected included the patients' behavior (aggressive versus non-aggressive), pulse rate, blood pressure, and weight change. Each patient's information was compared with the degree of exposure that patients had to the garden. They found patients who spent more than ten minutes in the garden per visit showed statistical improvements in all categories. The results were verified a year later when the study was conducted again.

Westphal stressed that patients' visits to the garden were "not part of an orchestrated program of horticultural activity."[9] They were not gardening or learning any information on gardening; their advanced condition would prohibit this. Yet, a ten minute experience with the garden was contributing something to patients' health, which is remarkable given that late-stage Alzheimer patients are thought to lose the ability to respond to their environment.

Lastly, the movement of our bodies is another important element of landscape experience that cannot be accounted for by ranking two-dimensional images. Damasio argues that cognition is not a phenomenon exclusive to the brain, but to our bodies, or what he calls the "somatic self." From our bones and muscles to the outlying regions of our skin, our somatic self tells us who we are and where we are, contributing to what we think and feel.

Since our bodies move there is an interaction between sensations and the movements of the body—sensorimotor activity. Much of this activity in our lives "does not depend on the conscious survey of the fact describing the task."[10] We don't consciously think to step up a flight of stairs. Rather this activity is learned and incorporated into our muscle memory. So aspects that regulate movement, such as a set of stairs, will add something to our impression of that experience. Stairs with wide treads and low risers, such as the Spanish Steps in Rome, or the narrow treads and impossibly steep risers, such as the steps of an Mayan pyramid, will make different impressions on the somatic self—as part of the experience.

This is an important distinction to make because much of the discussion of experience and evolution or even art and experience treats our bodies as motionless. However, we experience many landscapes through sensorimotor activity, such as climbing, walking, riding a bike, running, and the like.

Sensorimotor activity resides in our own unconscious learning, our muscle memory that has been in development since infancy. By six months of age, most people have developed a simple set of what developmental psychologist Jean Piaget called action schemes.[11] These actions are cause and effect scenarios, such as rolling a ball and watching it move, performed to experience the pleasure sense and that of motion. As children develop, these simple actions are tested and practiced until they are eventually paired together to perform more complex activities, such as hitting a ball with an implement, or imagining the ball as the world—experiences we call play.

Play experiences are integral to some of the basic precepts in human development, and there are over sixteen documented play types.[12] These types range from locomotor play that challenges strength and ability with no immediate goal, such as sledding down a hill; to creative play, such as building a city out of sand and water; to deep play that involves taking great risks, such as rock climbing. While these activities may be perceived as having no aim at all, actions in the experience of play are critical to dealing with real-life situations in children, and adults as well.

Play is useful to human development, but it is often performed for its own sake. Thus, it blurs the dichotomy of disinterestedness and instrumentality. While play was initially advocated for children, by the twentieth century the value of play as a basic human experience extended to adults—not as a need, but a right. This stimulated the creation of spaces specifically for play in Europe and North America. Today, playgrounds, dog parks, athletic fields, bike-ways, golf courses, and skate parks are landscapes that shape many of our daily experiences.

Parks accommodate not only the artifacts of play—the fields for organized sports, play equipment, and storage facilities—but sometimes the park's physical design itself can be a source of play. This is the case at Moerenuma Park, Japan. Moerenuma accommodates athletic activities such as baseball, track, and tennis—forms of play which provide their own aesthetic experiences for the performers and the audience. Yet, the park's unique land forms and spaces also encourage a play of the senses as the body moves through it.

Moerenuma Park[13]

Located on the outskirts of Sapporo Japan, Moerenuma attracts a wide age range of people, from art lovers, to thrill seekers, to sports enthusiasts. Its conceptual design was the work of landscape architect and sculptor, Isamu Noguchi, whose career has been defined by blurring distinctions between art and landscape, East and West, and formalism and surrealism. Before producing his popular Akari light series, Noguchi rose to fame in the 1960s with his design of sculptural landscapes for public parks, playgrounds, and plazas in North America. Tapping the sense perception of formalism and the collapse of conscious and unconscious realms of experience in surrealism, Noguchi showed us how a ramped form can magically become a slide, a work of art, a hill, and a prospect all at once.

In 1988 he was asked to redesign Sapporo's 16 hectare defunct garbage dump as Moerenuma Park. He finished the schematic design months before his death that year. The park did not open until 2005. Breaking with the small-scaled fastidious detailing of traditional Japanese landscapes, the park's colossal forms and spaces present the public with a cosmic composition of earth, stone, and water.

To the north lies a huge human-made mountain (Mt. Moerenuma) and a tilted amphitheater, flanked by sport facilities, and a giant tripod sculpture. To the south is the main gallery space and cafeteria, an animated Sea Fountain enclosed by a circular cedar grove, a beach, a pyramidal Play Mountain, and a series of human-scaled spaces that contain the play equipment Noguchi designed for mass production—such as his Slide Mantra, Jungle Gyms, and Play Modules.

On one hand this landscape is an exercise in memory because many of the Park's features reference Noguchi's past work. For example the huge Play Mountain has been compared to the sculptural landscape he proposed for a playground commission during the 1930s in New York City.

Figure 6.1 Isamu Noguchi, Moerenuma Park Mountain (photo credit: Dominic McIver Lopes)

Although his scheme was rejected by Parks Commissioner Robert Moses, Noguchi kept his maquette of the park, and today one can see striking similarities between the 1930s design and Play Mountain at Moerenuma. In fact, the gallery dedicates an entire section to a laborious retracing of the connections between Noguchi's past works and specific features of the park.

However, an experience with Moerenuma Park is more about what historian Robin Evans calls the "architecture of forgetting"[14]—a means to displace context and content. First, you forget that the park was once a garbage dump. The highly sculpted earth and stone forms and the strict geometry are more indicative of some neolithic settlement that never was, but now it has been improved by the present. Second, an experience of the park makes me immediately aware of the here and the now. Its extreme terrain and wide open vistas set against the big sky of Hokkaido accentuate the landscape's sensory qualities, creating an experience with literally space, form, air, color, and light.

Experiencing Moerenuma

In contrast to Japan's mainland, Sapporo's urban fabric is based on gridiron streets and large lots. Likewise, its buildings mitigate Hokkaido's cold weather with heaviness and impermeability rather than weightlessness and translucency, typical of the rest of Japan. Approaching the park by bus I catch glimpses of Mt. Moerenuma, which dwarfs the surrounding neighbourhood. Since three sides of the park are encircled by a river, it is only accessible by bridges. Once across, the vastness of the sky makes judging the scale of the earthworks impossible.

Unlike many parks, the circulation system at Moerenuma

does not guide my movement through the park to specific use areas—the basketball court, the picnic area, the fenced-off island of play equipment—the basic mental furniture of what we think a park is and contains. Instead, the forms and spaces themselves draw me to them, giving coherence to the park as one sculpture rather than a series of discrete outdoor rooms.

From the entry bridge the grass-covered Mountain is even higher than I imagined it would be. There is no visible main path up, so I begin anywhere. People are climbing all over the Mountain, and this is exciting because the movements of our bodies are often regulated by the design of a landscape—but here it is free from both the language and conventions of the path. With the will of the body against the forces of gravity and wind, people grapple with the Mountain in their own ways. Some run up it against the onward rush of people descending it. Elderly groups ascend the slope with a slow but steady pace, weaving around architects dressed in black who pause every few minutes to take a well composed picture. Then there are the children who roll down the hill with unbridled energy.

As I ascend the Mountain, both the velocity of the wind and the expanse of my view increases, until I look out over the City of Sapporo. I can also see the entire park below; the huge set of continuous steps that ascend Play Mountain, which is now dotted with people sitting to eat their bentos; the Amphitheater that hosts an impromptu ball game; the surge of water that is emanating from the Fountain much to children's shrill delight; and the beach where families linger and play in the sand at its watery edge. I also see the improbable meeting of these unique forms with the prescribed forms of play—the sports fields and ball courts. They are not separate from Noguchi's composition, but an integral component to it.

Due to the park's bold geometric forms and reduced material palette—stone, metal, water and earth, and plants—I am more sensitive to their presence and the way they interact with the light and wind. Biking through the park I am keenly aware that only by looking and moving do I start to make the visual connections between the lines and forms of the park with distant forms and shapes in and out of the park. For example, a massive retaining wall when viewed from one angle aligns with the lines of the giant pyramid and the silhouette of a distant mountain beyond.

Noguchi's play equipment area is the only part of Moerenuma that really tugged at my memory. Walking through this grove of small niches—each featuring one of his designs

Figure 6.2 Isamu Noguchi, Moerenuma Park Aqua Plaza (photo credit: Dominic McIver Lopes)

for play sculpture—is like walking through a history of childhood in the early 1970s. The vibrant colors, the playfulness of the forms, and the confidence we once had that children could encounter physical challenge is potently evident. I approach a Japanese father and his two sons who are playing with great excitement on a tangerine colored seesaw. They are actually from Kentucky. His sons have never played on a seesaw before.

There are numerous forms of play experiences at Moerenuma, from its organized play fields, beaches, sculptures, and the visual play of its forms. Yet, play is only one way in which we experience landscapes. Here I turn to Dewey who has outlined a framework for aesthetic experiences with art, which is highly relevant to experiences with landscapes. These are experiences that are not so much vested in our immutable quest for survival as evolutionary theories posits. Rather they are a point of departure for changing with time.

AESTHETIC EXPERIENCES
Everyday Experiences

Dewey's definition of an aesthetic experience privileges our experience *as an art* over the properties of an art object.[15] Thus, what we experience as art could involve an interaction with many things—a painting, novel, garden, basket, or rug, etc. Unfortunately, Dewey's definition lost value during the second half of the twentieth century because it was not pertinent in the Danto and Goliath battle to determine what was art. In fact Dewey's emphasis on experience clouds this debate over art. It was difficult to determine if Andy Warhol's *Brillo Boxes* (45 plywood boxes designed to resemble actual boxes containing steel wool cleansing pads) were art. Imagine trying to determine if an experience with the *Brillo Boxes* was art.

Nonetheless, Dewey's ideas bring a valuable perspective to understanding landscape experiences because he thought that aesthetic experience should be embedded in daily life and useful to us. Since landscapes are often the connective tissue of daily life—locating and structuring our homes, routes of travel, play, and work—our experiences with landscapes are prime sites for aesthetic experiences.

Philosopher Richard Shusterman argues that the banishment of aesthetic experience from everyday life has resulted in the "dismal assumption that ordinary life is necessarily one of joyless unimaginative coercion."[16] Moreover, this banishment "provides the powers and institutions structuring our everyday lives with the best excuse for their increasingly brutal indifference to natural human needs for the pleasures of beauty and imaginative freedom."[17]

This dismal assumption rationalized many of the inhumane transformations of urban landscapes created after World War II in the United States. Since art was relegated to the codified spaces of museums and theaters, landscapes that made up daily life—such as streets—were deemed unworthy of offering aesthetic experiences. For instance, the research of landscape architect Henry F. Arnold revealed that urban design in the 1960s and 1970s neglected to provide one of the most basic elements of human pleasure and comfort in our experiences with streets—trees.[18]

While we may not always be cognizant of their role in our experience and memory of an urban landscape, think of walking along the Champs Élysées in Paris, the Victoria Embankment along the Thames in London, or Memorial Drive in Cambridge, Massachusetts. These nineteenth-century landscapes are marked by the grandeur of their street trees and the spatial sensorial experiences they provide.

Unfortunately, Arnold found that when street trees were reintroduced into cities in the 1980s as poignant garlands to urban gentrification projects, neither their aesthetic functions nor science was considered. Emphasis was placed instead on perceived maintenance issues and short-term costs. As a consequence, small trees spaced widely apart were planted, resulting in statistics such as, the average life span of a tree in New York is seven years.[19]

Socialness

Philosopher Arnold Berleant posits that at the heart of an aesthetic experience—as well as what it means to be human —is the fully engaged, multi-sensory awareness of the world, and it is the "urban environment that holds the greatest possibility of achieving it."[20] For Berleant, humans are key participants in this experience; correlating with Dewey's theory that aesthetic experiences are a medium for socializing. These experiences have the ability to build relations between people, reinforcing both their individuality and identity as a group. Landscapes are often forums for social interaction. Parks, plazas, and courtyard gardens render the literal and figurative grounds for exchange. Thus, experience is neither exclusively internal or external, but a space between landscape and people.

Even in unofficial landscapes, for example, the spaces defined by the unrestrained skill and exuberance of skateboarders, are points for socializing. There is not only the aesthetic experience of skating, which creates strong social ties among the skateboarders, but for the bystanders watching their art as well. Although I don't think Dewey would have approved of rogue skateboarders, he held that aesthetic experiences were not about being "shut up within one's own private feelings and sensations."[21] They enable us "to share vividly and deeply in meanings to which we had been dumb . . . making common what had been isolated and singular."[22]

Also, many landscapes are inhabited locations, so experiences with these landscapes can accrue over decades, augmenting meaning through memory—a process that can lead them to having great significance. For example, when a small town in Missouri was forced to move after massive flooding, homeowners were funded by the federal government to move their houses to higher ground miles away. According to environmental psychologist Jamie Horwitz, who worked with the community in their move, many elderly people, some who had tended their domestic gardens for twenty to thirty years, could not stand to leave.[23] The move caused so much stress that some people refused the funding and stayed in the half abandoned town.

It's About Time

Dewey thought that significant aesthetic experiences must involve a set of phases that include experimentation, reflection, communication, and action—which are all driven by anticipation. We know that landscapes can play a powerful role in triggering memory, but on the oscillating side of memory is anticipation. It is the suspense of anticipation that molds the entire animation of experience. What we anticipate compels us to imagine, discover, and ultimately become satisfied, amazed, let down, or disillusioned by the experience.

Landscapes are spaces where our perception of time is fast-forwarded or slowed down, but landscapes are also never really finished. They change, and they don't always change exactly as we expect, and this is a dimension of their appeal from a small domestic garden to a city. This is where an understanding of landscape experience has much to learn from seasoned gardeners who have experimented, anticipated, and physically changed their gardens over time.

The work of garden artist Louis G. le Roy grasps this idea. For decades he has created gardens that capture the spaces between time, whether an instant or years. Time is not only marked by plant growth in his gardens, but also by the battle between plants as they compete with each other for sun, air, nutrients and space. In the 1970s he embarked on the creation of a 4 hectare landscape called Ecokathedraal in Mildam, Holland. This landscape introduces a third contender into the battle of space and time, le Roy himself. Racing against the time it takes for vegetation to battle it out and grow is the time it takes for him to build Ecokathedraal by hand. Thirty years later, a sumptuous landscape has emerged that mixes the madness of human will with the relentless fecundity of plant life.

In a sprawling landscape of walls, walkways, and platforms that appear to be losing the battle with plant growth, visitors are struck by the compulsion of seemingly continuous change. They also discover that there is another time indexed in le Roy's landscape, the city of Mildam. The non-plant material that comprises Ecokathedraal is construction debris from Mildam. le Roy has an agreement with the city's municipal government to receive this debris that is dumped on site on a regular basis by workers. With the continuous deposit of rebar, concrete rubble, and stones, each year's visit brings anticipation. In this sense, Ecokathedraal also captures the time it takes for Mildam to literally recycle itself, making the landscape both the abject remains of the city and the psychic terrain for renewal.

Anticipation in aesthetic experience is another way of thinking about the disinterested appreciation of landscapes

Figure 6.3 Louis G. le Roy, Ecokathedraal (photo credit: Peter Wouda/ www.timesfoundation.com)

Figure 6.4 Louis G. le Roy, Ecokathedraal (photo credit: Peter Wouda/ www.timesfoundation.com)

as still-life scenery—the appreciative mode that Carlson and Crandell condemn. Despite the fact that many national parks and scenic easements are designed and maintained to create scenes for viewing—camouflaging powerlines or the effects of logging along the way—there are still major transformations in the landscape, like fall color or spring blooms, that invite our anticipation and imagination.

For example, anticipation compels many people to travel long distances in the autumn to check out the chlorophyll levels in the leaves of trees. In 2004 approximately 7.7 million people visited the state of New Hampshire to witness fall colors. They may not be interested in the trees as sources of lumber or how various tree types are located in particular soils, but many are interested in change itself and the beauty it brings. We don't really know the exact time they will change, how long, how brightly, or in how much unison, but we can anticipate and imagine this—and this is an important way to experience landscapes.

While evolutionary theories would posit that the turning of leaves are pleasurable because it indicates it is time to prepare for winter, centuries of viewing paintings of autumn landscapes have helped cultivate our interest in this experience.[24] Likewise, the advent of technology, such as hand held cameras and other recording devices, have raised our awareness of landscape change, colored by anticipation.[25] Also, change and anticipation are not limited to biotic cycles. The past century has witnessed unprecedented alterations to landscapes—both to people's delight and disappointment.

Another subtle but powerful dimension of aesthetic experiences is adaptation. While anticipation heralds the new, what is yet to come, it can also signal us to adapt. In essence, our ability to anticipate change allows us to adapt. While evolution shapes innate genetic adaptations over large time spans, cultural adaptation is much faster and can happen within a lifetime. For example, in just a few decades we have accepted industrial artifacts as mnemonic elements in parks.

In this way, cultural adaptations are much more useful to us in seeing landscapes as landscapes. What matters about our experiences with landscapes is not that they match a hypothetical experience from our evolutionary past. What counts is the way landscapes engage us as part our quest to adapt and change with our own habits and human development. If we are people who only want to experience what we think our Pleistocene ancestors valued, we prevent growth and risk losing a very valuable human trait that is our ability to adapt and change with time. Our inability to adapt can effect our success in handling a range of landscape issues, from tolerating cultural difference to adjusting to climate change.

Keeping landscapes invisible distances us from the realities that shape them. But once we learn to see the invisible art, we find it everywhere, bringing art to daily experience—in the form of gardens, streets, plazas, playgrounds, neighborhoods, parks, and regions. The key is what the observer brings to the experience: there is more to seeing than mere *seeing*. Landscapes can be highly sensorial spaces, and since many landscapes are public, they can also provide important sites for social exchange. Some argue that the social capacity of landscapes will be replaced by a digital agora of on-line communities. However, it's more likely that the boundaries between physical landscapes and digital landscapes will be blurred.

Some landscapes accommodate virtual communities. At Bryant Park in New York, I can sit under the dappled light of London Plane trees and watch people, drink a coffee, and check my e-mail. Wireless internet built into the fabric of the park expands the traditional idea that parks should be publicly accessible spaces where people meet and interact.

Just as Bryant Park brings in the internet, the internet is a conduit to physical landscapes. With the aid of webcams, YouTube, and photo-sharing networks, I can observe landscapes rendered by ordinary people from all over the world. This puts a new twist on Jackson's idea that landscapes are created perceptually. For Jackson, salient components in this perception were roadways that connected people from different locations. He posited that "an essential element in any healthy political landscape is the network of neighborhoods and roads."[1] While Jackson referred to physical roadways, digital points of connectivity diversify the landscapes and people that we know and care about.

This unfolding may not come without costs. We cannot afford to ignore the fact that (like physical ones) digital landscapes are highly instrumental and not always benevolent. Moreover, just as physical landscapes are not solely the products of nature, digital landscapes are not created only by technology, but by people. Negotiating these challenges will mean casting a critical eye on landscape illusions and realizing rich landscape experiences in order to live from, with, and on landscapes.

Bibliography

INTRODUCTION

1 Tim Richardson, *The Vanguard Landscapes and Gardens of Martha Schwartz* (London: Thames and Hudson, 2004), p. 149.

2 Clemens Steenbergen and Wouter Reh, "The Tuileries Gardens," *Architecture and Landscape: the Design Experiment of the Great European Gardens and Landscapes* (New York: Prestel, 1996), pp. 215–235.

3 John Dixon Hunt, *Greater Perfection: The Practice of Garden Theory* (Philadelphia: University of Pennsylvania, 2000), p. 11.

4 Maggie Keswick, *The Chinese Garden: History, Art & Architecture* (New York: Rizzoli, 1980), p. 40.

5 Marc Treib, "Nature Recalled," *Recovering Landscape: Essays in Contemporary Landscape Architecture*, James Corner editor (Sparks, NV: Princeton Architectural Press, 1999), p. 29.

6 Hunt 2000, p. 212.

7 John Brinckerhoff Jackson, *Discovering the Vernacular Landscape* (New Haven: Yale University Press, 1984), p. 8.

8 Jackson 1984, p. 49.

9 This is an inversion of why many people value nature over art—that it is something which has not been produced for and/or by humans—something that we cannot change.

10 Jackson 1984, p. 8. The term landscape has had different meanings—often contested—in history and within different disciplines. There has also been much work involved in discerning different categories of landscapes—vernacular versus designed landscapes, for example. Jackson was mainly concerned with vernacular landscapes. However, his definition offers a very useful tool for analyzing all types of landscapes

because it introduces the idea of time, which opens up the definition of landscape to ideas about measure, structure, sequence, memory, and experience.

11 Art works, such as paintings, also require care; however, the sources of decay are exacerbated when a work, such as a garden, is outdoors.

12 Elizabeth Barlow Rogers, *Landscape Design: a Cultural and Architectural History* (New York : Harry N. Abrams, 2001), p. 78.

13 In addition to Kant's theory of disinterestedness, which he applied to free beauties, he also proposed a category of adherent beauties that acknowledges function and does not apply to the concept of disinterestedness. From a contemporary perspective, landscapes would seem to fall under adherent beauties; however, Kant appears to categorize landscapes with disinterestedness and free beauties. He mentions landscape gardens several times in *Critique of Judgment*, noting in his division of arts that landscape gardens fall under the category of painting. Even Kant finds this odd, stating that landscape gardening "actually takes its forms from nature (at least at the very outset: the trees, shrubs, grasses, and flowers from the forest and field), and to this extent is not an art whereas (say) plastic art is, {though it also exhibits its forms corporeally}—and the arrangement it makes has its condition no concept of the object and its purpose (unlike the case, say, architecture), but merely the free play of the imagination in its contemplation." See Kant Immanuel *Critique of Judgment*, Werner S. Pluhar trans. (Indianapolis, Indiana: Hackett, 1987) p. 323. Contemporary philosophers studying environments stress the disinterested appreciation of landscapes. Allen Carlson notes that "the historical roots of environmental aesthetics lie in the ideas about aesthetic appreciation developed in the eighteenth century and given classic expression by Kant. Central to this approach was the concept of disinterestedness, in virtue of which aesthetic experience was construed as distanced from daily interests, such as the practical and personal. The coupling of the concept of disinterestedness with eighteenth century fascination with the natural world resulted in a rich tradition of landscape appreciation." See Allen Carlson "Environmental Aesthetics" *The Routledge Companion to Aesthetics*, Berys Gaut and Dominic McIver Lopes editors, (New York: Routledge, 2002) p. 423.

14 Allen Carlson, "On the Theoretical Vacuum in Landscape Assessment," *Landscape Journal*, 12, (1) Spring 1993, pp. 51–56.

15 John Dewey, *Art and Experience* (New York: G.P. Putnam's Sons, 1958).

16 Dewey, 1958, p. 60. See also Michel Conan editor, *Contemporary Garden Aesthetics, Creations and Interpretations* (Washington D.C.: Dumbarton Oaks, 2007).

ONE   WHO DESIGNS LANDSCAPES?

1 Immanuel Kant, *Critique of Judgment* (translated by Werner S. Pluhar) (Indianapolis, Indiana: Hackett, 1987).

2 Larry Shiner, *The Invention of Art: a Cultural History* (Chicago: University of Chicago Press, 2001), pp. 147–148.

3 Horace Walpole, "The History of Modern Taste in Gardening," *The Genius of Place: The English Landscape Garden 1620–1820*, John Dixon Hunt and Peter Willis editors (New York: Harper & Row, 1975), p. 313.

4 Quoted from Albert Fein, *Landscape into Cityscape: Frederick Law Olmsted's Plans for a Greater New York City* (New York: Van Nostrand Reinhold, 1981), p. 398.

5 Linda Nochlin, "Why are there no great women artists?" *Women, Art and Power and Other Essays* (Boulder, Colorado: Westview Press, 1988), p.158.

6 Dianne Harris, "Cultivating Power: The Language of Feminism in Women's Garden Literature, 1870–1920," *Landscape Journal*, 13 (2) Fall 1994, pp. 113–123.

7 "The American Lawn: Surface of Everyday Life" was an exhibit held June 16 1998 to November 8 1998 at the Centre for Canadian Architecture in Montréal, Main Galleries, Octagonal Gallery, Hall Cases. It is also published in Elizabeth Diller and Ricardo Scofidio, "Docket", *The American Lawn*, Georges Teyssot editor (New York: Princeton Architectural Press, 1999).

8 Diller + Scofidio 1999, p. 208.

9 Vitaly Komar and Alexander Melamid, *Painting by Numbers: Komar and Melamid's Scientific Guide to Art*, JoAnn Wypijewski editor (Berkeley: University of California Press, 1997).

10 Arthur Danto, "Can It Be the "Most Wanted Painting" Even If Nobody Wants it?" *Painting by Numbers: Komar and Melamid's Scientific Guide to Art*, JoAnn Wypijewski editor (Berkeley: University of California Press, 1997), p. 124–139.

11 http://www.muf.co.uk/ahorsestale/, accessed April 30, 2007.
See also *THIS IS WHAT WE DO: a muf manual* (London: ellipsis, 2001).

12 http://www.muf.co.uk/ahorsestale/process.html, accessed April 30, 2007.

13 Light Source Lecture Series, *Gross Max*, Tuesday February 20, 2007, Vancouver.

14 The Library of Congress American Memory, "A Park is A Work of Art" *Today in History: April 26* (http://memory.loc.gov/ammem/today/apr26.html), accessed April 24, 2007.

15 Roland Barthes, *Mythologies*, Annette Lavers trans. (London: J. Cape, 1972), p. 38.

16 Wypijewski 1997, p. 19.

17 Jean-Jacques Rousseau, *Julie, Or the New Heloise*, Philip Stewart and Jean Vaché trans. (Hanover: University Press of New England, 1997), p. 394.

18 Jean-Jacques Rousseau 1997, p. 393.

TWO   WHAT CAN LANDSCAPES REPRESENT?

1 Leo Marx, *Machine in the Garden: Technology and the Pastoral Ideal in America* (New York: Oxford University Press, 1981), p. 116.

2 Denis E. Cosgrove, *Social Formation and Symbolic Landscape* (Madison: The University of Wisconsin Press, 1998), p. 13.

3 Quoted from Marx 1981 Thomas Jefferson, *Query XIX The present state of manufactures, commerce, interior and exterior trade?*, p. 124.

4 Karl Marx and Friedrich Engels. *Communist Manifesto*, Phil Gasper editor (Chicago: Haymarket, 2005).

5 Frederick Law Olmsted, *Walks and Talks of an American Farmer in England*, Charles C. McLaughlin, introduction (Amherst, MA: Library of American Landscape History, 2002), p. xxxii.

6 John Brinckerhoff Jackson, *The Necessity for Ruins and Other Topics* (Amherst, MA: The University of Massachusetts Press, 1980), p. 99.

7 Jackson 1980, p. 98.

8 Jackson 1980, p. 102.

9 Dean MacCannell, *Empty Meeting Grounds: the Tourist Papers* (London; New York: Routledge, 1992).

10 Nancy G. Duncan and James S. Duncan, *Landscapes of Privilege the Politics of the Aesthetic in an American Suburb* (New York: Routledge, 2004).

11 Leo Marx 1981, p. 131.

12 Duncan and Duncan 2004, p. 217.

13 Clemens Steenbergen and Wouter Reh, "Vaux-le-Vicomte," *Architecture*

Bibliography

and Landscape: the Design Experiment of the Great European Gardens and Landscapes (New York: Prestel, 1996) pp. 151–186.

14 Stephen Bann, "The Landscape Approach of Bernard Lassus," Journal of Garden History and International Quarterly 15 (2) April-June 1995, p. 69.

15 Gina Crandell, "Spectators of the Picturesque: Eighteenth-century England," Nature Pictorialized: "The View" in Landscape History (Baltimore: Johns Hopkins University Press, 1993).

16 Walpole, 1975, p.316

17 Robert L. Thayer, Gray World, Green Heart: Technology, Nature, and Sustainable Landscape (New York: Wiley, 1994).

18 http://www.hargreaves.com/projects/, accessed January 24, 2008.

THREE   ARE LANDSCAPES NATURAL?

1 Ludwig Wittgenstein, Wittgenstein's Philosophical Investigations, William H. Brenner trans. (Albany, N.Y. State University of New York, 1999) pp. 79–80.

2 Aldo Leopold, A Sand County Almanac (New York: Oxford University Press, 1966).

3 Freya Mathews, "Conservation and Self-Realization: A Deep Ecology Perspective," The Deep Ecology Movement, Alan Drengson and Yuichi Inoue editors (Berkeley: North Atlantic Books, 1995) p. 134.

4 Ibid, p. 133.

5 Kate Soper, "Nature/'nature," FutureNatural: Nature, Science, Culture, George Robertson, Melinda Mash, Lisa Tickner, John Bird, Barry Curtis, and Tim Putnam editors (London: Routledge, 1996) p. 32.

6 For a critique of bioregional mapping see Jonathan Olsen, "Region and "rootedness": Bioregionalism and Right-Wing Ecology in Germany, Landscape Journal 19 (1,2) 2000, pp. 73–83. For more examples in support of bioregional mapping see Mike Carr, Bioregionalism and Civil Society: Democratic Challenges to Corporate Society (Vancouver: University of British Columbia, 2004).

7 Stephen Jay Gould, "An Evolutionary Perspective on Strengths, Fallacies, and Confusions in the Concept of Native Plants," Nature and Ideology Natural Garden Design in the Twentieth Century, Joachim Wolschke-Bulmahn editor (Washington, D.C.: Dumbarton Oaks, 1997) p. 17.

8 http://www.earthfirst.org/about.htm, accessed April 27, 2007.

9 Soper, 1996, p. 28.

10 Edward Tufte, "Visual and Statistical Thinking," *Visual Explanations Images and Quantities, Evidence and Narrative* (Cheshire, Connecticut: Graphic Press, 1983) p. 27.

11 Charles Darwin, *The Origin of Species by Means of Natural Selection* (London: J. Murray, 1901).

12 Elizabeth Grosz, *Time Travels: Feminism, Nature, Power* (Durham: Duke University Press, 2005).

13 http://www.nps.gov/legacy/organic-act.htm, accessed April 17, 2007.

14 Malcolm Budd, *The Aesthetic Appreciation of Nature: Essays on the Aesthetics of Nature* (New York: Oxford University Press, 2002), p. 2.

15 Budd 2002, p. 17.

16 Budd 2002, p. 9, note 11. I refer to Budd here because he offers one of the clearest examples of what it means to appreciate nature. However, he ultimately argues against the moral arguments associated with appreciating nature.

17 See W.J.T. Mitchell, *Landscape and Power* (Chicago: University of Chicago Press, 1994).

18 Walpole 1975, p. 313.

19 Elizabeth Bohls, *Travel Writing, 1700–1830: an Anthology* (Toronto: Oxford University Press, 2005), p. 145–146.

20 Raymond Williams *Keywords A Vocabulary of Culture and Society* (New York: Oxford University Press), p.223.

21 Ronald Moore, "Appreciating Natural Beauty as Natural," *The Aesthetics of Natural Environments*, Allen Carlson and Arnold Berleant editors (Peterborough, Ont.: Broadview Press, 2004), p. 218.

22 Moore 2004, p. 219. This point is also discussed by Christian Helmut Wenzel. He notes that Kant uses hearing the songs of a nightingale bird as an example. We might feel elevated by this language of nature, but this is ruined when we discover that "we have been deceived by "a mischievous lad who knew how to imitate this song." " See Christian Helmut Wenzel, *An Introduction to Kant's Aesthetics* (Oxford: Blackwell, 2005) p. 114.

23 Johann Georg Sulzer "Landscape (art of design)" *General Theory of Fine Arts 1771–4* in *Art in Theory 1648–1815 An Anthology of Changing Ideas*, Charles Harrison, Paul Wood, and Jason Gaiger editors (Oxford: Blackwell, 2000), p. 841.

Bibliography

24 Joris-Karl Huysmans, *Against the Grain (A Rebours)*, Havelock Ellis trans. (New York: Hartsdale House, 1931), p. 104.

25 Huysmans 1931, p.186.

26 Gert Groening and Joachim Wolschke-Bulmahn, Die Liebe zur Landschaft Teil III. Der Drang nach Osten. Zur Entwicklung der Landespflege im Nationalsozialismus und während des Zweiten Weltkriegs in den "eingegliederten Ostgebieten," HERLYN, Ulfert und Gert Gröning (Hg.): Arbeiten zur sozialwissenschaftlich orientierten Freiraumplanung Band 9, Minerva-Verlag, München, 1987. Gert Groening and Joachim Wolschke-Bulmahn "The ideology of the nature gardens. Nationalistic trends in garden design in Germany during the early twentieth century" *Journal of Garden History* 12(10)1992, pp. 73–80. Gert Groening and Joachim Wolschke-Bulmahn, "Some notes on the mania for native plants in Germany" *Landscape Journal* 11 (2) 1992, pp.116–126.

27 Johannes Zechner "Ewiger Wald und Ewiges Volk—Der Wald als nationalsozialistischer Idealstaat" *Naturschutz und Demokratie!?*, Gert Groening and Joachim Wolschke-Bulmahn editors (Muenchen: Martin Meidenbauer, 2006), pp. 115–120.

28 Gert Groening and Joachim Wolschke-Bulmahn, "The National Socialist Garden and Landscape Ideal, Bodenständigkeit (Rootedness in the Soil)" in *Art, Culture, and Media, Under the Third Reich*, Richard Etlin editor (Chicago: University of Chicago Press, 2002) pp. 73–97. For expansion of Landscape Rules into Poland see Gert Gröning, "Der Überfall auf Polen und seine Auswirkungen auf das Konzept der deutschen Landespflege" *Planung in Polen im Nationalsozialismus* (Berlin: Hochschule der Kuenste Berlin, 1996), pp. 91–105.

29 Kiran Klaus Patel, "Konvergenz von Demokratie und Diktatur?" *Naturschutz und Demokratie!?*, Gert Groening and Joachim Wolschke-Bulmahn editors (München: Martin Meidenbauer, 2006), pp. 183–191.

30 Aldo Leopold, "Notes on Game Administration in Germany," *American Wildlife*, 25 (6) 1936, pp. 85, 92–93.

FOUR   MEMORY AND EMOTION

1 Quoted from George Dickie, *The Century of Taste: The Philosophical Odyssey of Taste in the Eighteenth Century*. Archibald Alison, *Essay on the Nature and Principles of Taste* (1790) (New York: Oxford University Press, 1996) p. 61.

2 Stephanie Ross, *What Gardens Mean* (Chicago: University of Chicago Press, 1998), p. 179.

3 Richard Payne Knight, *An Analytical Inquiry into the Principles of Taste* (London: Printed by Luke Hansard for T. Payne and J. White, 1805). For further discussion see Stephanie Ross, "The Picturesque: An 18th Century Debate" *The Journal of Aesthetics & Art Criticism*," 45 (2) 1987, pp. 225–227.

4 Knight, 1805, p. 348.

5 Thomas Whateley, *Observations on Modern Gardening* (1770) in *The Genius of Place: The English Landscape Garden 1620–1820*, John Dixon Hunt and Peter Willis editors (New York: Harper & Row, 1975), p. 307.

6 Udo Weilacher, *Between Landscape Architecture and Land Art* (Basel, Switzerland: Birkhauser, 1999), p. 122.

7 Weilacher, 1999, p. 129.

8 Gas Works Park by Richard Haag is another early example of an industrial conversion to park land that retains many of the structures as part of its design. See Elizabeth K. Meyer "Seized by Sublime Sentiments Between Terra Firma and Terra Incognita" *Richard Haag: Bloedel Reserve and Gas Works Park*, William S. Saunders editor (New York: Princeton Architectural Press; Cambridge, Mass.: Harvard University Graduate School of Design, 1998).

9 Antonio Damasio, *The Feeling of What Happens: Body and Emotion in the Making of Consciousness* (New York: Harcourt Brace, 1999), p. 39.

10 The Quinnipiac University Polling Institute in Hamden, Conn., 74 percent said it is very important or somewhat important to see signs of progress at the World Trade Center site. http://www.newsday.com/news/printedition/newyork/nyc-nypoll134700626apr13,0,5022307.story?coll=nyc-nynews-print, accessed April 13, 2006.

11 James O. Young, "Memory and Counter Memory," *Harvard Design Magazine Constructions of Memory on Monuments Old and New*, Fall 1999, p 12.

12 Harriet Senie, "Mourning in Protest," *Harvard Design Magazine Constructions of Memory on Monuments Old and New*, Fall 1999, p. 27.

FIVE   INSTRUMENTAL IMAGINATION

1 Tony Bennett, Lawrence Grossberg, Meaghan Morris, *New Keywords A Revised Vocabulary of Culture and Society* (London: Blackwell, 2005), pp. 178–179.

2 Paul Harris, *The Work of the Imagination* (London: Blackwell, 2000).

3 Kevin Lynch, *Image of the City* (Cambridge: M.I.T. Press, 1960).

4 Lynch, 1960.

5 Jackson, "The Domestication of the Garage" (The University of Massachusetts Press, 1980), pp. 103–111.

6 Jackson 1980, p. 107.

7 Jackson 1980, p. 108.

8 Shikibu Murasaki, *The Tale of Genji*, Arthur Waley trans. (New York: Random House, 1960). Katsura also makes references to specific views in Japan, such as Amanohashidate—a narrow strip of land connecting two opposing sides of Miyazu Bay.

9 Murasaki, 1960, p. 342.

10 See John Beardsley, *Earthworks and Beyond: Contemporary Art in the Landscape* (New York: Abbeville Press, 1998) and Udo Weilacher, *Between Landscape Architecture and Land Art* (Basel, Switzerland: Birkhauser, 1999).

11 John Beardsley, "Artists" Statements", *Earthworks and Beyond: Contemporary Art in the Landscape* (New York: Abbeville Press, 1998), p. 133.

12 Matthew Potteiger and Jamie Purinton *Landscape Narratives* (New York: John Wiley & Sons, 1998).

13 Clare Copper Marcus, "Unexpected company: a redesigned urban square attempts to serve the needs of Oakland's homeless community and downtown office workers," *Landscape Architecture Magazine* June 2003, http://www.asla.org/lamag/lam03/june/feature1.html, accessed April 29, 2007.

14 Noel Caroll "On Being Moved by Nature: Between Religion and Natural History" and Allen Carlson, "Appreciation and the Natural Environ- ment" *The Aesthetics of Natural Environments*, Allen Carlson and Arnold Berleant editors (Peterborough, Ont.: Broadview Press, 2004), p.93.

15 Carlson, 2004, p. 64.

16 Friedrich Froebel, *The Education of Man*, W. N. Hailman trans. (New York: D. Appleton, 1906), p. 257.

17 Susan Herrington, "The garden in Frobel's kindergarten: beyond the metaphor," *Studies in the History of Gardens and Designed Landscapes* 1998 18 (4), pp. 326–338.

18 Amanda Reeser and Ashley Schafer, "Lifescape: Field Operations," *Praxis Landscapes*, 2002 (4), pp. 20–28.

19 William James, "Will," *The Principles of Psychology* (New York: Henry Holt

and Company, 1905). See also John M. Capps and Donald Capps, *James & Dewey on Belief and Experience* (Chicago: University of Illinois Press, 2005), pp. 93–110.

SIX AESTHETIC EXPERIENCE

1 Jay Appleton, *The Experience of Landscape* (New York: Wiley, 1996).
2 Rachel Kaplan, Stephen Kaplan, and Robert L. Ryan, *With People in Mind: Design and Management of Everyday Nature* (Washington, D.C.: Island Press, 1998). See also Stephen Kaplan "Environmental Preference in a Knowledge-Seeking, Knowledge-Using Organism," *The Adapted Mind Evolutionary Psychology and the Generation of Culture*, Jerome H. Barkow, Leda Cosmides, and John Tooby editors (New York: Oxford, 1992), pp. 581–598.
3 Gordon H. Orians and Judith H. Heerwagen "Evolved Responses to Landscapes' " *The Adapted Mind Evolutionary Psychology and the Generation of Culture*, Jerome H. Barkow, Leda Cosmides, and John Tooby editors (New York: Oxford, 1992), pp. 555–579.
4 Gordon H. Orians, "An Evolutionary Perspective on Aesthetics," *American Psychological Association, Psychology of Aesthetics, Creativity, and the Arts*, http://www.apa.org/divisions/div10/articles/orians.html, accessed April 30, 2007.
5 Danto, 1997.
6 Denis Dutton, "Aesethetics and Evolutionary Psychology" *The Oxford Handbook for Aesthetics*, Jerrold Levinson editor (New York: Oxford University Press, 2003), http://www.denisdutton.com/aesthetics_&_evolutionary_psychology.htm, accessed June 15 2007.
7 David Hume, *A Treatise on Human Nature*, translated by Lewis Amherst Selby-Bigge (Oxford: Clarendon Press, 1978), p. 265.
8 Alan Hirsch, "Nostalgia: A Neuropsychiatric Understanding,"' Association for Consumer Research Annual Conference, Chicago, Illinois, October 19, 1991.
9 Lauren Spiers, "Landscape Design Is Just What the Doctor Ordered Dr. Joanne Westphal, ASLA, discusses therapy gardens at the National Building Museum" *Land Online*, April 18, 2005, http://www.asla.org/land/041805/westphal.html, accessed April 30, 2007.
10 Antonio Damasio, *Descartes' Error: Emotion, Reason, and the Human Brain* (New York: Avon Books, 1994).
11 Jean Piaget, *Play, Dreams, and Imitation in Childhood*. C. Gattegno and F. M. Hodgson Transl. (New York: W. W. Norton, 1962).

12 Bob Hughes *A Playworker's Taxonomy of Play Types* (London: Playlink, 2002).

13 Moerenuma Park was completed under the direction of the Isamu Noguchi Foundation, architects Shoji Sadao and Junichi Kawamura, Kitaba Landscape Planning, Park Director Hitoshi Yamamoto, and city officials. Noguchi's overall concept was carried through and some details were designed based on previous projects by Noguchi. For example, the Aqua Plaza shown in the photograph is thought to be an interpretation of "California Scenario," a well known plaza in Costa Mesa, California. Here it is interpreted for children's play and it was very popular during my visits.

14 Robin Evans, Mies Van der Rohe's, "Paradoxical Symmetries," *Translations from Drawings to Buildings and Other Essays* (Cambridge, Massachusetts: MIT Press, 1997), p. 268.

15 Dewey 1958.

16 Richard Shusterman, "Pragmatism: Dewey" *The Routledge Companion to Aesthetics*, Berys Gaut and Dominic McIver Lopes editors (New York: Routledge, 2002), p. 102.

17 Shusterman, 2002, p. 102.

18 Henry F. Arnold, *Trees in Urban Design* (New York: Van Nostrand Reinhold, 1993).

19 Arnold, 1993, p. 147.

20 Arnold Berleant, "Cultivating an Urban Aesthetic," *The Aesthetics of Human Environments*, Arnold Berleant and Allen Carlson editors (Peterborough, Ontario: Broadview Press, 2007), pp. 79–80.

21 Dewey 1958, p. 25.

22 Dewey 1958, p.244.

23 Jamie Horwitz, "Leaky Walls" *Thresholds* 20, *Be-Longing* Spring. (Cambridge, MA: The MIT Press, 2002), pp. 30–34.

24 Enjoying the changes in color of leaves could be disinterestedness.

25 John R. Stilgoe *Landscape and Images* (Charlottesville: University of Virginia Press, 2005), pp. 299–300.

ENVOI

1 Jackson, 1984, p. 37.

Index

genius artist concept 20
Germany 66–7, 78, 86
Goldsworthy, Andy 69–70
Gould, Stephen Jay 56–7
Grand Tour 72
Greeks, ancient 9–10, 72, 101
Groening, Gert 66–7, 139n26
Gross Max 28–30
Grosz, Elizabeth 60

Han Dynasty 6
Hargreaves Associates 50–1
Harris, Paul 92, 93
Heerwagen, Judith 112
Henry V 71–2
Hestercombe 15–16
High Line, Manhattan 81–3
historic landscape 37–8, 39
history/narrative 95–8
Hoare, Henry II 73–4
Hood, Walter 103–4
Horwitz, Jamie 126
human intervention 4–5, 32, 49,
    58, 63
Hume, David 114–15
Hunt, John Dixon 4, 7, 103
Huysmans, Karl 65–6

idealism/reality 35–6, 47–9
ideology 36–7, 63, 66–8
imagination 9; instrumental 10–11,
    92–4; narrative 93–5, 105–6;
    play 91–2; structural models
    106–9
impermanence of life 88
Inclosure Acts 63
indigenous landscapes 36, 55

industrialization 53–4, 93–4, 130
infrastructure landscapes 50–1
internet 131–2
invisibility of landscape 131

Jackson, J.B. 7–8, 9, 36–7, 84–5,
    94–5, 131–2
James, William 110
Japanese gardens 3–4, 5–6, 8,
    96–8, 118–23
Les Jardins de Métis 14–15
Jastrow, Joseph 52, 53
Jefferson, Thomas 34, 38
Jekyll, Gertrude 15–16

Kant, Immanuel 138n22; artists 20,
    23; Critique of Judgment 17,
    134n13; disinterestedness 11,
    134n13; nature/morality 65
Kaplan, Rachel and Steven 111–12
kare-sansui (dry gardens) 3
Katsura Rikyu Imperial Villa 96–8
Kent, William 17–18, 44, 64, 76–7
King, Martin Luther 37
kirei sabi aesthetic 97–8
Knight, Richard Payne 74–5, 105
Komar, Vitaly 24–6, 111

Lafayette Square, Oakland 104
land ethic 54
land use 26, 34, 63–4
landscape: as artifice 16; authorship
    of 4–5, 108; myths 5–6, 31–2,
    55; nature 5, 6–8, 31, 62–4,
    68–70; valued 92–3
Landscape Architecture 2
landscape painters 42–4